•Bartholor

WALK DĿVON & CORNWALL

by David Perrott and Laurence Main

Bartholomew

A Division of HarperCollins*Publishers*

CONTENTS

British Library Cataloguing in Publication Data
Perrott, David
  Walk Devon & Cornwall.
  1. Devon – Visitors' guides 2. Cornwall – Visitors' guides
  I. Title II. Main, Laurence
  914.23504859
  ISBN 0–7028–1283–8

Published by Bartholomew,
a Division of HarperCollins*Publishers*,
Duncan Street, Edinburgh EH9 1TA

First Published 1991
© Bartholomew 1991

ISBN 0 7028 1283 8

Printed in Great Britain by Bartholomew,
HarperCollins*Manufacturing*, Edinburgh.

Produced for Bartholomew by
Perrott Cartographics, Darowen, Machynlleth, Montgomeryshire.
Typesetting by Perrott Cartographics and Litho Link.
Litho origination by Litho Link, Welshpool, Montgomeryshire.

Britain's landscape is changing all the time. While every care has been
taken in the preparation of this guide, the authors, Perrott
Cartographics and Bartholomew, accept no responsibility whatsoever
for any loss, damage, injury or inconvenience sustained or caused as a
result of using this guide.

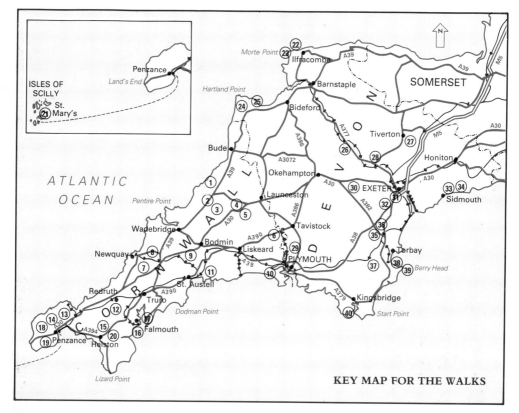

KEY MAP FOR THE WALKS

Key to the maps

Scale 1:25000

All the maps are drawn on a north axis, ie. with north at the top

═══════	Major road	┼┼┼┼┼	Railway (private)	▲	Summit
───────	Other road	Ⓐ	Description in text	81m	Spot height in metres
‑‑‑‑‑‑‑	Track or footpath	❋	Viewpoint	🅿	Parking
‑ ‑ ‑ ‑	Route of walk		Woods or forest	🚌	Bus stop
─■─	Railway (BR)		Cliffs or crags		

WALKING IN DEVON AND CORNWALL

Devon and Cornwall are Britain's premier holiday counties. They occupy the most south-westerly part of England, a peninsula enclosed by the Atlantic Ocean and warmed by the mild waters of the Gulf Stream to an extent that palm trees thrive in the open.

The coast has been battered by fierce winter gales into a series of irregular bays, many enclosing fine sandy beaches, others providing sheltered havens for fishing craft. Here you will find quaint harbours and picturesque villages.

Inland, narrow wooded valleys, rich with plants and wildlife, spill down from wild expanses of moorland. Everywhere there are the relics of an ancient past – standing stones, stone circles, holy wells and churches. Cornwall is an old Celtic Kingdom where King Arthur and his knights were thought to have roamed, but history and legend have become so entwined that even the historians cannot agree!

The walks in this guide have been carefully chosen to introduce all these facets of Devon and Cornwall. None of the walks are particularly difficult, many are very easy, and there is always ample interest for both the casual and experienced walker. For those who then wish to explore further, there are other titles in this series. *Walk the Cornish Coastal Path* by John Mason (which covers the entire Cornish section of the South West Way), *Walk Dartmoor* by Peter Tavy and *Walk Exmoor & The Quantocks* by Lyn Rivers, cover specific parts of Devon and Cornwall in great depth. There is so much good walking to enjoy here, you will surely wish to thoroughly explore all of these areas.

1 THE LANDSCAPE OF DEVON

Devon has plenty of room for walkers, being the third largest county in England, after North Yorkshire and Cumbria. Its southern coastline is occupied by the major towns of Plymouth, Torbay and the fine capital city of Exeter, separated by smaller resorts, fine sandy beaches and rocky coves. Barnstaple is the only fairly large town in the north, although small market towns and villages are scattered around. Devon is famous for the red soils around Exeter, but this New Red Sandstone is only part of a varied pattern which adds interest to the scenery. In the east of the county young Cretaceous Greensands form plateaux, while the south coast has chalk cliffs as it approaches Dorset. In the north, the rocks are Carboniferous. Limestone is found with shales and slate in the south.

Rivers dissect this landscape, with the Tamar forming the border with Cornwall. The Exe flows a long way from Exmoor through a broad wooded valley to Exeter. The Torridge flows inland from the Hartland peninsula to join the Taw at its mouth. The latter flows northwards from Dartmoor. Most of the rivers that rise in Dartmoor flow southwards into deep, drowned estuaries along the south coast, as with the Dart and the Teign.

Woodland and vast acres of rolling farmland lie between Exmoor and Dartmoor. South of Dartmoor the well-drained soil supports arable farming as well as providing pasture. Cider, a favourite local drink, is made from apples grown in the east.

2 THE LANDSCAPE OF CORNWALL

Cornwall is now classified as a county, but it was once a Celtic nation, like Brittany or Wales. Its spirit is hard and resistant like the rocks that form this sea-girt land. The Lizard peninsula reveals the oldest rocks dating from the lower palaeozoic age, some 400 million years ago. Most of Cornwall is formed of Devonian strata, plus some Carboniferous grits in the north. Granite was intruded into these by volcanic action, from Bodmin Moor westwards to Hensbarrow Downs, Carnmenellis, West Penwith, and the Isles of Scilly, 25 miles (40 km) out to sea. This granite, revealed by millions of years of weathering and erosion, rises out of a plateau to form Cornwall's spine. River valleys cut deeply into this, while rias, or drowned river valleys, are a characteristic of the coastline. The River Fal is a classic example.

The landscape is often windswept and treeless, although the mild winters allow exotic plants to flourish in sheltered places. Woodlands do exist in the valleys, and the hedgerows harbour colourful flowers. The wildest place is Bodmin Moor, with its rocky summit tors and boulder-strewn flanks. Cattle, sheep and ponies graze the coarse grasses, bracken and heather. Brown Willy is the county's highest point at 1377 feet (420 m). In the west, the changeable maritime climate brings the clear light much loved by artists.

3 A SHORT HISTORY OF DEVON

Devon contains a great number of prehistoric remains, especially on Dartmoor. When the Romans arrived, they found this to be the territory of the Dumnonii tribe. They seem to have come to an understanding with this tribe, and there are no signs of conflict. Instead, the fine city of Isca Dumnoniorum (Exeter) was built. The Celtic kingdom of the Dumnonii was re-established when the Romans withdrew, but the Saxons gradually took over the best farming land. Devon was absorbed by them by about 700, and it is Saxon place names which predominate today. Alfred the Great set up four boroughs – Barnstaple, Exeter, Lydford and Halwell – in the 9th century, later replacing Halwell (which lost its borough status) with Totnes.

The Celts used the prehistoric ridgeways, which are still important routes, but it was the Saxons who imposed the local paths and lanes, using them to link farms, mills, villages, salt pans and lime kilns. A sharp bend is an indication of a field boundary that had to be respected – indeed many paths were formed out of boundary ditches. The Norman Conquest made little difference to the affairs of this far flung shire. The Cistercians, when they came, built Buckland Abbey, took Buckfast from the Benedictines and introduced sheep farming. The woollen and cloth industries brought prosperity to places like Tiverton and Exeter from the 13th to the 18th centuries.

The growth in international trade led to the development of ports and shipping. By the time of the Spanish Armada, Devon had bred such famous mariners as Sir Francis Drake, Sir Walter Raleigh, Sir John Hawkins, Sir Humphrey Gilbert and Sir Richard Grenville. Devon fishermen began fishing off the coast of North America in the late 16th century, and the tradition continued until the early 20th century. The speech of the people of Newfoundland betrays their Devon origins. Devon people colonised other parts of North America, notably Virginia. Some of those who stayed at home worked in the Navy base at Devonport. Founded in the late 17th century, this was to become the largest employer in the south-west and the home of what was once the most formidable fleet in the world.

4 A SHORT HISTORY OF CORNWALL

A very large number of ancient monuments, such as stone circles, isolated standing stones and stone-capped quoits, remarkable for their profusion at the extreme western tip of Cornwall, suggest that this was a place of great ritual significance some 4000 years ago. Many of these stones line up with each other to form excellent examples of what are either ley (earth energy) lines, or ancient alignments, depending on your point of view. One such famous alignment runs from St. Michael's Mount over the cheesewring on Bodmin Moor and right across the country via Brentor, on Dartmoor, to Glastonbury Tor and Avebury.

Cornwall has many churches dedicated to Celtic saints who predate St. Augustine, the first Archbishop of Canterbury who was sent from Rome in AD597. Legend states that Jesus came here with his uncle, Joseph of Arimathea. Joseph was a tin trader, and Cornwall was famous for its tin in ancient times, making the legend more credible. St. Just in Roseland is one of the places where Jesus is said to have set foot.

The Romans left Cornwall very much alone and it formed part of the revived Celtic kingdom of Dumnonia after the Romans departed in AD410. Cornwall has links with the Arthurian story through characters such as Sir Geraint, although English romantic writers, including Lord Tennyson, mistakenly located some Arthurian sites here.

The Saxons eventually gained nominal control over Cornwall in the ninth century, but it wasn't long before they were themselves displaced by the Normans.

Throughout Cornwall's recorded history tin has been extracted, initially from the alluvium of streams, and later, from mines. Stannery courts and a parliament were set up early in the 13th century to regulate the industry.

During times of economic depression and social unrest, the Cornish were never afraid to express their discontent. Over 15,000 Cornishmen marched on London in protest at being taxed to pay for a war in Scotland in 1497. Later the same year, 6,000 Cornishmen, together with the French and Scottish, rallied behind Perkin Warbeck, an imposter who claimed to be the younger son of Edward IV and who made a false claim to the throne of England. In 1549 the Act of Uniformity, which introduced the First English Book of Common Prayer, sparked off another rebellion. This imposition of the English church service was the death knell for the Cornish language, contrasting with the effect of the translation of the Bible into Welsh in 1588, and the subsequent safeguarding of that Celtic language. The last Cornish speaker, Dolly Pentreath, died in 1778, although enthusiasts are now reviving the language.

Meanwhile, Cornwall's mines, with copper now more important than tin, were booming. A crucial factor in this boom was the use of steam power and various inventions, especially the beam engine for pumping, winding and crushing ores. As foreign competition closed the mines in the late 19th century, many Cornish miners emigrated, spreading their expertise around the world. Today, the landscape of Cornwall is littered with empty engine houses. Methodist chapels are invariably found nearby, a reminder of the hold John Wesley's preaching had on the miners. China clay, or kaolin, is still vitally important to the Cornish economy.

5 THE ISLES OF SCILLY

These are a group of about 100 low lying islands and islets about 28 miles south-west of Land's End, Cornwall. Their climate is influenced totally by warm Atlantic winds and the Gulf Stream, which bring mild winters, early springs and warm, dry summers, enabling many sub-tropical plant species to thrive.

Surrounded by clear, shallow seas, the islands were, before the coming of man, joined to the mainland. It was probably this that led to the islands being thought of as the legendary 'Lost Land of Lyonesse', in the sequel to the story of King Arthur. After Mordred killed Arthur, Arthur's followers were pursued across Cornwall, finally reaching the western hills. Following their arrival the land between these hills and Land's End was submerged, drowning Mordred's army

The islands contain the most south-westerly fresh water pool in Britain, a vital resource for migrating birds. Annet is the premier sea bird breeding island in the group, supporting significant populations of puffin, storm petrels and Manx shearwater. Seals breed around all the islands.

6 WILDLIFE

The lanes of inland Cornwall are aglow in summer with foxgloves, red campion and other colourful flowers. Where there are ancient woods, usually in the valleys, the dominant tree is the sessile oak, with some ash and holly. These support mosses, ferns, fungi and lichens, including the large plate-shaped tree lungwort. This indicates the relative lack of pollution in the air. Look out for orchids in the boggy moorlands. Heather and gorse are plentiful. The clifftops of Devon are carpeted in wild flowers. The colours range from pink thrift to the blue of spring squill and the yellow of golden samphire.

Otters still inhabit the rivers of both counties. The River Torridge, in Devon, was once the home of Tarka the Otter, the hero of Henry Williamson's famous book. Nowadays the introduced mink is more common. Guillemots nest on the cliff ledges. Rock pools may reveal hermit crabs at low tide.

The mudflats of the estuaries attract wading birds and wildfowl. During the winter the River Exe is home to thousands of Brent geese from arctic Russia. The avocet, emblem of the RSPB, also visits. The rich woodlands of the river valleys are home to the wood warbler, while the pied flycatcher and the redstart are other summer visitors. Kestrels, buzzards and ravens can be seen, although the chough is now extinct in Cornwall.

7 CLOTHING AND EQUIPMENT

These walks enable you to enjoy walking without having to make an expensive investment in lots of clothing and equipment. The clifftop paths have been made safe for the many tourists who visit Devon, and the wilds of Bodmin Moor are, during the summer, within most people's capabilities. Old green lanes and field paths are a fascinating aspect of British walking for the experienced, as well as a gentle introduction for the newcomer. All of these walks can be completed during the summer in sensible ordinary shoes, training shoes or wellingtons. If you intend to explore the uplands during the winter months, you will need a good pair of walking-boots.

The south-west of England usually receives a fair amount of rain, so do take a good anorak with you. Waterproof over-trousers are essential in winter. Gloves and a hat, such as a balaclava, are also recommended for winter walking. Spare clothing should always be carried.

A light weight rucksack is the best way to carry the things you need on a walk. A small one will do for a short walk, but it must have room for some food and drink, such as dried fruit, nuts or chocolate, and water. An emergency first-aid kit of patches, antiseptic cream and pain-relieving tablets should be standard equipment, along with a torch and spare batteries. Take the relevant map and a good compass and practise using them on friendly terrain. Note that where approximate distances are given in walk directions, the metric equivalents are also approximate; eg. 100 yards or 90 metres.

8 RIGHTS OF WAY

These walks are along established rights of way. Please remember always to keep to the path and regard it as a privilege, as well as a right, to follow it across someone else's land; in that way we can build an atmosphere of co-operation rather than confrontation in the countryside. If you have a dog, please ensure that it does not foul the footpath, and *keep it on a lead*. The Animals Act (1971) states that dogs considered to be a danger to livestock may be shot. The Protection of Livestock Act (1953) makes it an offence to permit a dog to worry livestock, with a maximum fine of £200.

Access to the countryside is becoming more and more vital as a means of relaxation in a hectic society. In theory, your rights are well protected by the law but, in practice, some paths become obstructed. Most people don't like to follow obstructed paths, so these become neglected and targets for extinguishment. Please report any obstructions you may find to the local highway authority, which is the respective County Council.

Obstructions should also be reported to: The Ramblers' Association, 1/5 Wandsworth Road, London, SW8 2XX. Tel. 01-582 6878.

9 THE COUNTRY CODE

Enjoy the countryside and respect its life and work.
Guard against all risk of fire.
Leave gates as you find them.
Keep your dogs under proper control.
Keep to public paths across farmland.
Use gates and stiles to cross fences, hedges and walls.
Leave livestock, crops and machinery alone.
Take your litter home.
Help to keep all water clean.
Protect wildlife, plants and trees.
Take special care on country roads.
Make no unnecessary noise.

10 USEFUL ADDRESSES

Car parking information is given for each walk. British Rail can also be used to reach the start of several of them. Others can be reached by bus, but please do check these services *before setting out*. Using public transport is the rambler's way of safeguarding the countryside from having yet more roads built. It is also important to support public transport since, for some, it is the only means of access to the countryside. Ask at your local British Rail station about bargain weekly rover or day ranger tickets. There are similar bargain tickets on the buses.

For information on buses in Cornwall, contact: Cornwall County Council, County Hall, Truro, TR1 3BJ, Tel. 0872 74282.

For bus information in Devon contact: Devon County Council, County Hall, Topsham Road, Exeter, EX2 4QW, Tel. 0392 382070.

Both counties are covered by the:

West Country Tourist Board
37 Southernhay East, Exeter, Devon, EX1 1QS, Tel. 0392 76351.

There are local Tourist Information Centres in many of the major towns and resorts.

South West Way Association
This was formed in 1972 with the aim of furthering the interests of walkers on the 570 miles of Great Britain's longest long-distance trail. Details from: Eric Wallis, Secretary, Windlestraw, Penquit, Ermington, Ivybridge, Devon, PL21 0LU, Tel. 0752 896237.

Walk 1

BOSCASTLE

5.5 miles (8.9 km) Moderate

This is a romantic walk through shady trees and beside a swirling young river in the Valency Valley. When Thomas Hardy, the great Wessex novelist, came here, he met and fell in love with Emma Lavinia Gifford, the girl with 'nut brown hair, grey eyes and rose-flush coming and going'. This is a walk in their footsteps, to the church which Hardy restored.

A Allow time, if you can, to explore Boscastle. This village was once an important port, having the only sheltered harbour in 40 miles (64 km) of rugged coastline. Its name is derived from the Botterels or Bottreaux family, from Angers in France, who built a motte, or mound, nearby in about 1080.

The railway didn't reach north Cornwall until 1893, so the local slate was being exported from here by sea in Hardy's day, in exchange for coal and limestone from South Wales and general merchandise from Bristol. In stormy weather, you may see a spectacular geyser of spray from the 'blow hole', by walking out to the small stone quay at the harbour mouth – **but take care**. There is a Museum of Witchcraft near the harbour, which is open daily Apr - Jun & Oct 10am - 5.30pm, Jul - Sep 10am - 8.30pm. Admission charge.

B Somewhere in the Valency River, below one of its miniature waterfalls, Hardy lost a picnic tumbler. Recalling the event after Emma's death, he wrote the poem *Under the Waterfall*:
'By night, by day, when it shines or lours,
There lies intact that chalice of ours,
And its presence adds to the rhyme of love

Persistently sung by the fall above.
No lip has touched it since his and mine
In turns therefrom sipped lovers' wine.'
He also sketched the scene.

C This white-washed cottage may be the model for Widow Jethway's home in Hardy's novel *A Pair of Blue Eyes*.

D St. Julietta's church in St. Juliot was founded by St. Julitta, one of the 24 saintly daughters of King Brychan, who ruled over the Brecon area of South Wales in the early sixth century. The parish has now been amalgamated with six others, but it lives on in Hardy's writings as West Endelstow. A sketch in the church shows the 'six-and-thirty old seat ends' that Hardy noted before his restoration work removed them.

E The Old Rectory (now a private house and not open to visitors) is where Hardy first met Emma. She recalled 'a blue paper sticking out of his pocket . . . . He had a beard, and a rather shabby greatcoat, and had quite a business appearance . . . . the blue paper proved to be the manuscript of a poem, and not a plan of the church'. Hardy was here in his capacity as an architect to plan the restoration work on the church, having arrived from Launceston railway station on 3rd March, 1870. He only stayed four days, but returned for a longer stay that August. Emma had been here since 1868, when her sister, Helen, married the vicar and she moved in as the couple's housekeeper. Hardy was to make more visits and to write *A Pair of Blue Eyes* here (the novel was published in May 1873). Hardy proposed to Emma in this 'little paradise of flowers and trees' and they were married in London in September 1874. Hardy returned after Emma's death in 1912 and recollected how they had sat in the garden discussing news of the Franco-Prussian War whilst a man with an 'old horse pulling a harrow' worked in the field below. This simple scene was to open the famous poem *In Time of The Breaking of Nations*.

F Minster's dramatically situated church dates from the 15th century and was renovated in the 19th century. A Benedictine monastery stood here from the 12th century until 1386, built on the site of a fifth-century hermit's cell.

G Peter's Wood used to be managed as a coppice. The steep valley sides have allowed the survival of the original deciduous trees, such as oak.

Over

BOSCASTLE

1 Boscastle is on the B3263, 4.5 miles (7.2 km) to the north of Camelford. Start from the car park in the centre of the village. Buses stop at the nearby Wellington Inn (203 from Bude, 204 from Tintagel, 212 from Launceston, 213 from Plymouth and 242 from Bodmin).
Go right from the car park along the pavement of the B3263 towards Bude. Soon turn right through a small gate to enter the National Trust's Valency Fields. Follow a meadow path to a small gate in the left hand corner ahead.

2 Go ahead with trees on your left and a meadow, then a river, on your right. Continue through a gate at the neck of the field to walk along a shady path beside the river on your right. This is the Valency River and you keep it on your right as you pass a meadow on your left. Go through a kissing gate in the field corner ahead and continue along the shady, riverside path to reach a footbridge on your right. Do not cross it now but note that you will return over it. Go ahead, still with the river on your right, into the National Trust land at New Mills.

3 Pass a cottage on your left, then ignore a lane on your left but go ahead along a waymarked path. Continue through a gate with the sign 'Footpath to St. Juliot Church'. About 20 yards (18m) further on, fork left up a narrow path signposted ' Public Footpath St. Julietta's Church'. Go through a gate and along a steep bank. Pass a ruined cottage on your right and emerge through a kissing-gate beside a signpost in the corner of a field. Go ahead, as waymarked, beside a hedge on your left.

6 Look for the roof of a church down on your right. Turn right just before it to follow a signposted path. Go through a gate into the National Trust's Peter's Wood, Minster. Follow this path down to a fork and bear left into woodland. Your path is soon joined by one coming from the left. Go downhill through the trees to a footbridge. Cross this to return to your outward path. Turn left to retrace your steps back to Boscastle.

5 Bear left with the track to a corner of a field and descend beside a hedge on your right. Go through a gate and straight downhill back to the signposted crosspaths. Turn right back to New Mills, with the hedge now on your right, to retrace your steps. Turn left after following the path along the steep bank, to cross the river by a footbridge (with a ford on your left). Take a gate ahead to go up a hedged track to a lane. Bear right to a road junction, where you turn right towards Boscastle.

4 Go straight ahead at a signposted crosspaths, towards St. Julietta's Church. Go through a gate in the corner and cross a field to a waymarked slate stile. Go over this and bear right, keeping close to a hedge on your right. Ignore a gate in this hedge and continue to a stile in the corner ahead. Cross this to follow the waymarked path, walking with a hedge on your right. Go ahead over a stile in the next corner, and bear left uphill to cross a stile into the churchyard. Leave by the path to a lane, where you turn left. Pass Penventon Farm on your left, then turn left down a track. Ignore a path through a gate on your right, then pass the Old Rectory on your right.

CAMELFORD

4 miles (6.4 km) Easy

A quiet riverside walk leads to an isolated old church south of Camelford. The River Camel was mistakenly believed by Tennyson to be where King Àrthur fought his last battle, but the Saxons did defeat the Cornish at nearby Slaughter Bridge in the ninth century. Look out for heron and kingfisher.

1 Start from the bus stop near the library and the Methodist church in Camelford, which is on the A39 between Bude and Wadebridge. This is served by buses 202 (Bude to Truro), 212 (Tintagel to Launceston), 213 (Boscastle to Plymouth), 242 (Boscastle to Bodmin), 245 (Tintagel to Newquay) and 246 (Tintagel to Camelford). Cars can be parked at the roadside nearby. With your back to the Methodist church and facing the Liberal Club, go left along a lane between Barclays Bank and the library. Climb almost to the top of the hill before turning left to visit the museum.

2 Retrace your steps downhill to the library and go right up Fore Street. Just before a shoe shop on your left, turn left along a passage signed 'Public Footpath to the River and Advent Church'. Follow the path beside the River Camel, which is now on your left. Cross a footbridge so that the river is on your right, then cross a second footbridge to continue with it again on your left. Go ahead, ignoring a third bridge, to reach a lane which crosses a stone slab bridge on your left.

3 Turn right to follow the lane uphill. Pass a signposted path on your right then turn left through the second gate on your left after it, along a signposted path. Walk beside a hedge on your left to cross a stile beside a gate in the field corner ahead. Continue across a field and over a stile into woodland. Emerge at the corner of a field and maintain your direction to a footbridge. Cross this and veer left to a gate leading to a road.

4 Go right along the road. Pass Trethin Manor on your left and veer left over a stile to take the signposted path to Advent Church. This passes a duck pond on your right, crosses a stone slab bridge and a stile before veering left to the church. Leave through a gate and along an access track to a lane. Turn right along the lane.

5 Fork right opposite Viddy Vu (a bungalow on your left). Go right at the next road junction, where there is a letterbox.

6 Continue past a telephone box on your left, ignoring a road on your right. Reach a T junction and go left for 20 yards (18 m) then turn right through a small metal gate and veer right down to a footbridge. Go across and climb up the field to its top right corner, where you cross a slate stile to the left of a gate.

7 Turn right and immediately fork left to pass a farmhouse on your right. Bear left at a crosstracks, going ahead through a gate and along a hedged track. Emerge at the corner of a field and descend to its bottom right corner to go through a metal gate and cross a footbridge. Veer left to cross a stile. Continue uphill to cross a stile beside a gate. Bear right along a lane leading from the stile to the A39. Go left back to the start.

Camelford   A39

Pencarrow

River Camel

A39

Tresinney

B

A

A The North Cornwall Museum and Gallery has exhibits covering many aspects of local life, including cidermaking. A moorland cottage has been reconstructed as it appeared about 1900. Open Apr - Sep Mon - Sat 10.30am - 5pm. Admission charge.

B Advent church may be named after St. Athwanne, one of the 24 daughters of the sixth-century Welsh king Brychan.

ROUGH TOR

3 miles (4.8 km) Strenuous

0 ————————————————— 1 mile
0 ————————————— 1 km

This is a very pleasant walk on a clear day, when fine views reward you for a fairly strenuous ascent. Bodmin Moor is the wildest place in Cornwall and Rough Tor is its second highest spot at 1311 feet (400 m). The ridge is impressively rough, being littered with huge slabs of granite which have been dramatically weathered. There is peace, solitude and the sound of skylarks.

1 *Start from the Forestry Commission and North Cornwall District Council car park. This is below Rough Tor at the end of a lane, Roughtor Road, which leaves the A39 on the northern edge of Camelford and leads over 2 miles (3.2 km) south-eastwards to the high moorland.*
With the forest on your left and the tors ahead, go ahead through a kissing-gate at the bottom of the car park.

2 *Cross a slab bridge over a stream and go ahead up a faint, grassy track. Veer left towards Showery Tor, a rocky outcrop on your far left. This is surmounted by a 'cheesewring', a rock feature. Turn right along the ridge to Rough Tor, with its magnificent views.*

4 *Retrace your steps to the bridge, go left across it and climb back up to the car park.*

3 *Descend to the end of the ridge and turn right back towards the car park. Pick up a fence on your left which guides you down to the bridge. Just before the bridge, turn left to see the monument.*

To Camelford

P

C Monument

Settlement

B

Showery Tor

Little Rough Tor

Rough Tor A

A Across the moorland to the south-east Brown Willy can be seen, the highest spot in Cornwall at 1375 feet (420 m). Rough Tor isn't much lower at 1311 feet (400 m). In the opposite direction a vast china clay pit is visible. Powerful streams of water here separate the china clay in decomposed granite from the accompanying quartz and mica. The result is a pure white mud, which is dried in long, heated sheds. The china clay is exported and the waste quartz is left in large heaps.

A medieval chapel dedicated to St. Michael once marked Rough Tor's summit, which now bears a plaque in memory of the 43rd (Wessex) Division, who trained here. Their sacrifices during World War II prompted Sir Richard Onslow, the former landowner, to present this land to the National Trust in 1951, in their memory. The plaque faces a logan-stone, a rock poised to sway at a touch. A basin may have been scooped out of its top to contain a beacon fire or sacrificial blood. In areas of china clay extraction look out for the blue of amethyst quartz in moorland streams.

B Look out for Bronze Age (1800 BC) oval enclosures and hut circles here. The enclosures were paddocks made with stones cleared from the fields.

C The monument is a granite column erected by public subscription in memory of a young servant-girl, Charlotte Dymonde, who was murdered here on Sunday, 14th April, 1844, by a fellow servant, Matthew Weekes.

POLYPHANT

0 _____ 1 mile

0 _____ 1 km

2.5 miles (4 km) Easy

This is an excellently waymarked and maintained route which takes you across meadows and pasture, then along an old green lane to a Methodist chapel. It starts from the village green, which is an unusual feature in Cornwall, where most villages tend to be linear. The name Polyphant means 'Pool of the Frog'. Local granite quarries originally brought prosperity, and this has continued, with the village quadrupling its size since 1945.

5 *Turn right (left if you have just come down the lane from the bus stop at Pipers Pool) over a stile beside a gate to follow a signposted path. Walk with a hedge on your left up a long field to cross a stile in the top hedge 20 yards (18 m) to the right of the corner.*

6 *Veer right to a gap, cross the top of the next field and take an old green lane all the way to a road junction where Polyphant Methodist church is situated. Go left along the road for 30 yards (27 m), then turn right down a signposted path which veers right to lead to The Green, with its telephone box.*

1 *Polyphant is just off the A30, 5 miles (8 km) west of Launceston. Cars can be parked at the roadside. The nearest bus services stop at Pipers Pool on the A395, 5 miles (8 km) west of Launceston. These are nos 74 (Launceston to St. Austell), 212 (Tintagel to Launceston) and 213 (Boscastle to Plymouth). If you arrive by bus, take the lane for 1 mile (1.6 km) south from here to join this route at no **5**.*
Start from the village green, and with the telephone box on your left, bear right along the diagonal road. Ignore a lane ahead but turn right up a concrete track to pass Bowden Derra Park Private Home on your left.

To Pipers Pool 1 mile (1.6 km)

Trethinna

Ⓒ

Ⓑ Trerithick

Polyphant

Bowden

Ⓐ

4 *Go left for 200 yards (180 m) along the road to a footpath sign on your left pointing across the road. Turn right here up a concrete track to a farmyard and bend left, then right, with it as waymarked (ignoring a path on your left). Go ahead through a metal gate. Reach an old field boundary on your left and an avenue of trees on your right. Ignore a gate on your left but continue with a hedge on your left to cross a stile in the field corner. Go down steps to a road, go left for 20 yards (18 m) then turn right at a road junction. Follow the road for 350 yards (320 m) to pass Trethinna.*

3 *Go ahead to a farmyard where you turn right as directed by a yellow arrow, then go left to a waymarked gate. Go through this and veer slightly right across a field to cross a wooden stile. This leads to a slate stile in the wall and another wooden stile on the other side. Cross both. Go ahead across a very long field to cross a wooden stile in its far corner. Continue over a step stile in the wall ahead to reach a road.*

2 *When the access track to Bowden Derra bears left, fork right along the waymarked rough track, soon crossing another access drive to the house. Go ahead along a waymarked old green lane to a gate in the corner of a field. Continue beside a hedge on your right to a gate in the next corner.*

A Bowden Derra was once the manor house. The present building dates from 1866 and has a staircase of Polyphant stone. The local school sports used to be held in the grounds, but the building is now a private home.

B Trerithic Farmhouse was built between 1575 and 1595.

C Trees now cover the old disused quarries. Polyphant stone was used in many ancient churches and in Launceston castle. It also featured in the Great Exhibition of 1851.

```
0                                                    1 mile
|----|----|----|----|----|----|----|----|----|----|
0                              1 km
```

This attractive, waymarked route is called 'White's Way', because it goes across or near land owned by three unrelated families called White. There are splendid views from the hilltop, and the area's long history is confirmed by the ancient inscribed Ogham stones to be seen inside and outside the church.

> **1** Start from St. Martin's Church, Lewannick. This village is 5 miles (8 km) south-west of Launceston, from where there is an infrequent bus service (no 216, Tuesday mornings only). There is a car park opposite the church beside the Archer Arms.
> Go left, passing the church on your left. Turn right at a signpost to go through a farmyard. Take the waymarked gate ahead to follow at first a fence, then a wall, on your right.

> **2** Continue through a gate in the field corner to follow a field boundary (an overgrown earth bank surmounted by a fence) on your left. Pass a bench on your left, facing the magnificent view on your right.

> **3** Continue through the kissing-gate in the field corner ahead. Walk with the field boundary still on your left. Cross a waymarked stile in the next corner and veer slightly left downhill to a gate in the bottom left corner of the field.

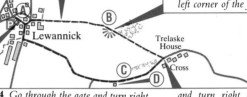

Lewannick

Trelaske House

Cross

> **4** Go through the gate and turn right along a road. Ignore a road on your left in order to return to the village and turn right to return to the church.

A The name Lewannick may be derived from Llan (sacred enclosure) of St. Winoc or Wethenoc. The parish church of St. Martin is built on an ancient site. Further evidence of early Celtic Christianity is in the shape of two Ogham stones. Ogham was a form of writing made by cutting notches along the edges of stones. It is at least as old as the fourth century AD and probably originated in southern Ireland. The script represents the letters of the Roman alphabet with short strokes cut in groups. It went out of fashion in the 7th century. One Ogham stone can be seen in the churchyard behind Mrs Thomas' headstone (a big Cornish cross). This is on your left as you enter. It may be the older of the two, in poorer condition and only marked in Ogham. The second stone is kept inside the church at the back, under the tower. This is marked in both Ogham and Latin. It may be a memorial to a local king. The church was built on land given in the early 13th century to Launceston Priory by Richard, Lord of Trelaske. It was rebuilt in the 15th century, when the tower was constructed of local Polyphant stone. Fire destroyed most of the rest of the building in 1890 but it was rebuilt in the same perpendicular style. The Norman font, with its geometrical patterns, survived the fire, and there is a new oak screen with painted panels of St. George and St. Martin.

B Not only is this a well waymarked path, but the Parish Council has thoughtfully provided you with a seat from which to admire the view south from Beacon Hill! Caradon TV mast can be seen in the distance, over 6 miles (9.6 km) away. Fox Tor can be seen on your right (west) and the whole area on the far side of the River Lynher (Lyn meaning lake, her meaning long) has many Bronze Age hut circles.

C Trelaske Court was built in the 18th century as stables for the nearby Trelaske House. The last of the Archers, the Lords of the Manor who built it, died in 1958 and the estate was broken up. The village pub recalls their name.

D The recently restored Keeper's Cottage.

0   1 mile
0   1 km

This delightful walk beside the River Tamar brings you to within a stone's throw of Devon. The steep climb through ancient woodland will reward you in the autumn with a fine display of fungi. You can travel to the start of this walk by train along a scenic branch line from Plymouth. Luckily, when the railway system was pruned in 1966 only the line west of Gunnislake was closed.

5 *Turn left, and left again at a junction with a road. Go right at a T junction to pass a telephone box on your right. Ignore a road on your left and a signposted path on your right. Continue to the A390 and turn left downhill and round a bend. Go left up Chawleigh Close back to the British Rail station.*

1 *Start from Gunnislake station, the terminus of British Rail's Tamar Valley Line from Plymouth. Cars can be parked here. Gunnislake is served by buses 622 and 623 from Tavistock.*
Go left along the station drive to the A390. Turn left under the railway bridge and go right up Well Park Road for 100 yards (90 m), then turn left down a road towards the River Tamar.

2 *Bear right at a junction, continue for 300 yards (275 m), then fork left down a signposted public footpath. Turn left at the bottom to walk with the river on your right.*

4 *Reach a gap in the corner of a stone wall on your left at the top of the ridge. Go left through this and along a narrow path to emerge at a signpost on a lane beside houses on your right.*

3 *Keep to the riverside path until you reach a road bridge. Go ahead across the road, keeping the bridge on your right, to pass an old garage on your left. Ignore gates on your right and bear left up a metalled track into woodland. Reach a signpost, ignore steps on your left, but fork left at the waymark post ahead to pass Hawkmoor Cottage on your right. Take a fairly steep narrow path up a wooded ridge.*

New Bridge

Gunnislake

Drakewalls

Station

A390

A Notice the old lime kiln where this route joins the bank of the River Tamar. The river was the main transport artery until the late 19th century and this section was canalised. Medieval fish traps were sited at the weir, which also marks the junction between fresh and salt water.

B Newbridge was built in 1520 and was the lowest road bridge crossing of the Tamar until the completion of the Saltash Bridge in 1962. Its seven arches carry a narrow road which, as the principal entry into Cornwall, was fought over in the Civil War.

C A miners' hostel once stood on the site of this old garage.

D The oak, hazel and willow of this ancient wooded common conceal the remains of the Gunnislake Clitters mine. This was an important area for tin, copper, arsenic and wolfram in the early 19th century. Mining ceased in the 1920s.

E The railway first came here in 1872 as the narrow gauge East Cornwall Mineral Railway, from Kelly Bray, west of Gunnislake, to Calstock Quay. In 1908 it was re-laid to Plymouth as a standard gauge line.

EAST WHEEL ROSE

2.5 miles (4 km) Easy

This is a gentle walk along country lanes and an attractive woodland path, passing the site of the most important lead mine in Cornwall.

East Wheel Rose is now owned by the Lappa Valley Railway and a trip on this is highly recommended, as it will also provide access to Churchtown.

the impressive ruined engine house that can be seen from the woodland path. The station at Benny Bridge is not far from this route.

1 *The bus stop is at the crossroads in the centre of St. Newlyn East. Services run here from Truro (86 and 280) and Newquay (51, 52, 86 and 280). Cars may be parked beside the parish church, down*

Churchtown.
Facing the church, turn left to pass the Pheasant Inn and walk to the right, then fork right along Metha Road.

2 *Reach a signposted path to Nanhellan through the trees on your right. You will take this path, but first go ahead along the road a further 100 yards (90 m) to view the Lappa Valley Railway from a bridge across it. Go back to the signposted path and walk along it through the trees and beside a stream on your left.*

To Benny Bridge
A
Church
P
St. Newlyn East
B
Lappa Valley Railway
Ventonarren Farm
C
East Wheal Rose

3 *Cross stone and wooden stiles to emerge from the wood. Bear right to go through a metal field gate and up a farm track to a road.*

4 *Turn right along the road and keep right at a junction to return to St. Newlyn East.*

A The parish church of St. Newlyn East contains a list of the names of its vicars since the 13th century. The village takes its name from the Celtic St. Newlyna. In tradition she was a British princess who arrived here from Ireland. She struck her wooden staff into the ground and said 'Let a church be built'. The fig tree growing out of the south wall of the church is supposed to have sprung from this staff. There is a legend that anyone who harms this tree is doomed to die within a year. St. Newlyna herself was beheaded in this area by her own father when she refused to comply with his planned marriage for her. When the head of a 15th-century Lantern Cross was discovered in the churchyard recently (it is now kept near the font), it depicted the saint with her head in her arms.

B The Lappa Valley Railway provides a 2 mile (3.2 km) ride along a 15 ins (37 cm) gauge track behind a steam engine. Trains run

daily from Easter to October, starting from Benny Bridge. This is 1 mile (1.6 km) north-east of St. Newlyn East (turn right as you face the Pheasant Inn and fork left, as signed). It occupies part of the old line from Newquay to Chacewater, which was opened in 1905 and closed in 1963. This section is older, having started as a horse-drawn tramway between Newquay and East Wheel Rose in 1849. Bought by the Cornwall Minerals Railway in 1873, it was converted for use by steam locomotives and incorporated into the Newquay to Chacewater line.

C Lead and silver, rather than the usual tin and copper, were the attractions at East Wheel Rose. The first shafts date from 1812 and the mine was thriving by 1823.

The quality of the lead and silver fell as the mine was dug deeper, however. A decline in the price of lead saw this mine abandoned in 1832. The valley of the little River Lappa became the home of a new mining venture in 1834 which proved more successful. The quiet stream was transformed into a noisy, hissing, bustling place which employed over a thousand men, women and children. East Wheel Rose was regarded as an extremely dangerous mine in which to work, and was the scene of the worst disaster in Cornish mining history. A total of 38 miners were drowned in July 1846, when a cloudburst flooded the lower workings. The most powerful pumping engine in Cornwall failed to prevent the mine finally closing in 1885.

COLAN

4 miles (6.4 km) Moderate, but muddy in places

Country lanes, tracks and field paths combine to make this a peaceful walk. There is some attractive woodland, a view over a reservoir and a visit to an ancient church, as well as a holy well. The return to Mountjoy is along a quiet road which affords fine views over Newquay and the coast. As the eastern end of Porth Reservoir is a nature reserve, you will probably see many birds, with waders common in the winter.

6 Turn right along the access lane. Go through a gate and turn right towards Tregoose. Descend to cross a bridge near the old mill and climb to a T junction. Go right, towards Colan. At the next junction, turn left towards Newquay. This road takes you back through Mountjoy to the bus stop.

5 Go ahead over a stile beside a gate to enter woodland. In the woods, ignore a track going left. Glimpse Porth Reservoir on your left, then go ahead across a bridge. Cross a boggy patch and bear right uphill to reach a farm access lane near the trees on the hilltop.

4 Turn left along the road to reach Colan church. Follow the road around past the church on your right. When the road turns sharply left, go straight ahead along a track.

3 Retrace your steps over the concrete blocks back to the field. Go left, through another wooden gate. Follow a clear path across a field to a gateway. Continue with a hedge on your left and through a gate in the corner to go ahead along a track.

2 Turn right along a lane for a few paces to see the Lady Nance Well down on your right.

1 Start · from the bus stop at Mountjoy, on the A392, 4 miles (6.4 km) east of Newquay. This is served by buses 21 (Newquay to St. Austell) and 91 (Newquay to Truro). Cars can be parked considerably in Mountjoy.
Take the signposted road to Colan. Bear left down a track to pass St. Joseph (a cottage) on your right. At the track's end go left over a stile beside a gate and descend to a small wooden gate on the left, in the left hand field corner. Go through this and cross a stream. Continue along a path made of concrete blocks.

Over

A The waters of Lady Nance Well were once famous for curing eye ailments. On Palm Sunday the locals cast palm crosses into the well to see if they would survive the year. The portents were bad if their cross didn't float. Nance is related to the Welsh word nant, meaning a stream or brook.

B St. Colan is an interesting name for a church. It may be derived from the Celtic St. Collen, who served for a while as Abbot of Glastonbury. A church at Llangollen in Wales is also dedicated to him. St. Colan may well be linked to an ancient fire deity, as the name is Cornish for coal and the saint's festival is held in May, close to the time of Beltane, another ancient festival celebrated with fire.

C Porth Reservoir was opened in 1960 to supply Newquay with water.

D Ochre used to be mined here.

E A mill has stood on this site since at least 1562. The wheel was only removed during World War II, when it was needed for scrap iron.

St. Colan's church

LUXULYAN

4 miles (6.4 km) Moderate, but can be muddy

This fine walk along the narrow wooded valleys of Luxulyan is packed with interest. Many of the paths are alongside artificial water-courses, or leats, and industrial archaeology abounds. Nature lovers will be delighted with the variety of natural deciduous trees and plants.

1 Luxulyan is clearly signposted off the main A390 road at St. Blazey. There is good roadside parking opposite the church. If you arrive by train, turn left out of the station approach road, and right at the T junction to reach the church.

With the church on your left walk down the hill and out of the village. After crossing a small bridge over a stream, turn right along a lane signposted 'Luxulyan Valley'.

2 When a lane joins from the left, go ahead between granite posts, then bear left through trees for about 50 yards (45 m) to climb a small embankment containing a leat (watercourse). Walk with the leat on your left for about 1 mile (1.6 km).

3 About 130 yards beyond the remains of a waterwheel, the track of the old incline passes obliquely over the leat. Walk downhill to your right to visit Ponts Mill. Return by the same route following the course of the old incline uphill. It curves to the left to join another leat parallel to, but above, your outward path. Follow the path beside the upper leat.

5 Turn right onto a wider path to cross a bridge over a leat, followed by a stone stile. Walk along a distinct green track to a granite post on your left. Look for stone steps over a wall on your left 20 yards (18 m) beyond this, and climb over. Walk along the righthand side of a field. Luxulyan village appears ahead. Go through a gateway, cross a track and enter a second field. Now follow the obvious path back to the church.

4 As the leat goes underground, the Treffry Viaduct appears straight ahead. Cross it and walk ahead with a leat on your right. About 125 yards (115 m) after the path crosses another leat, look out for steep steps which descend to your left. Go down. A short tunnel appears to your right. Follow the path *away* from the tunnel. Pass a small shed to your left, and after 10 yards (9 m) cross two small footbridges.

A This holy well is dedicated to St. Cyor.

B Granite sleepers lie embedded in the ground on the Carmears Incline, opened in 1841, where trucks carrying crushed minerals from Ponts Mill were pulled up the 1 in 10 slope by wire rope.

C Planned by Joseph Thomas Treffry, the Treffry Viaduct was built in 1839.

D The church of Sts. Cyriacus and Julitta in Luxulyan is a fine 15th-century building constructed from local granite.

PORTWRINKLE AND SHEVIOK

3.5 miles (5.6 km) Easy, but can be muddy

This is a gentle walk from the rocky foreshore along a charming sunken lane and around the narrow valleys of Sheviok, to rejoin the coast above the tiny tidal harbour of Portwrinkle. There is an excellent view over Whitsand bay, and the hedges are rich in summer with crab apples, brambles, sloes, dog rose, honeysuckle, damson and hawthorn.

4 *Immediately before a big open barn on the left, turn left through a metal field gate. Walk down a field with a wire fence on your right. Cross the stile at the bottom and turn left. Follow the path, with a high bank to your left. Continue over a stile, a footbridge and another stile to rejoin Trewrickle Lane.*

3 *Turn left off the road, following a sign indicating 'Tredis ¾'. When the road forks, walk downhill to the left, ignoring the next sign to Tredis. You pass the bungalow 'Woodlands'. Continue along the lane for 900 yards (820 m).*

2 *When the path joins the narrow tarmac Trewrickle Lane at a squeeze stile, continue ahead along the lane, ignoring a public footpath sign to the left. At a crossroads, turn sharp left, opposite Stumps Cross. Walk carefully along this road for 300 yards (275 m).*

5 *Turn right and follow the tarmac lane to a T junction (ignoring your earlier path off to the left). Turn right. Walk 100 yards (90 m) and, before the dark green bungalow, turn left down a lane signed 'Unsuitable for motors'. Follow this past the tiny harbour and back to your car.*

Trewrickle Farm
B
Stumps Cross
Trewrickle Lane
Saunders Lane
A
B3247
B3247
The Bungalow
Portwrinkle
Golf course
Harbour
Obelisk
Finnygook Beach

1 *This walk starts in Portwrinkle, which is signposted off the B3247 coast road at Crafthole. Park in the seafront car park just beyond the Whitsand Bay Hotel.*
With your back to the sea, walk to the right below the hotel, ignoring the white gated path but turning left at the public footpath sign. Walk uphill through the golf course car park, to follow the narrow waymarked path in the far corner. This is Saunders Lane. Follow this path, carefully crossing the B3247 and continuing ahead.

A Saunders Lane takes its name from the lime-rich sand that was carried along it to be spread on to the naturally acid soil of the surrounding fields. Its high banks provide shelter for a host of wild flowers, hedgerow fruits and butterflies.

B There has been a farm at Trewrickle for at least 800 years.

C The tiny tidal harbour at Portwrinkle (which was originally Portwrickle) was built jointly in the 17th century by the father and son Carew and the parishioners of Sheviok, creating a prosperous community based on pilchard fishing. When the fishing failed in the 19th century, the village died with it. The Whitsand Hotel once stood at Torpoint, and was known as Thankes Manor. It was moved stone by stone to its present site in 1909.

Walk 11

GOLANT

3.5 miles (5.6 km) Easy

The River Fowey is at its most beautiful when passing Golant, and this walk initially follows a path with sufficient height to give spectacular views over the wooded slopes and moored yachts. Sheltered lanes are taken inland until again the river valley comes into view by St. Sampson's church. Part of this route follows the Saint's Way (*Forth an Syns* in Cornish), a path crossing Cornwall from Padstow in the north to Fowey in the south.

A Golant was known as Golenanta in the 15th century, and means the fair in the valley. It is a picturesque village of small cottages around the Fisherman's Arms pub, and rises steeply behind a tidal anchorage enclosed by a railway line. This line, which carried passenger trains to Golant Station until the 1960s, is still in use, but only for the transport of china clay to the docks above Fowey. The old quay, which once served trading craft, is now surrounded only by yachts and dinghys.

B There is a fine view up Penpoll Creek. Just out of sight, about 800 yards (725 m) up this inlet, is St. Cyric's Creek, where the Priory of St. Cadix once stood, founded by the Welsh missionary, St. Cadoc.

C Bodmin Pill (also known as Sawmills Creek) was used as a tidal harbour by the merchants of Bodmin in medieval times, who wished to avoid paying harbour dues at Fowey. Pill is a Celtic word signifying a tidal creek.

D Looking south-east, the mound on the skyline at the head of the valley is Castle Dore, an iron age earthwork.

E This road is the driveway to Penquite Youth Hostel, which is situated in a fine Italianate stucco mansion built circa 1840 by Colonel Peard. One of Colonel Peard's friends was the Italian politician Garibaldi, who stayed here in 1864.

F St. Sampson's church stands in a superb elevated position overlooking the River Fowey, built beside a holy well which is now enclosed to the left of the porch. Its founder, Sampson, who was born in Glamorgan in the sixth century, was the son of Amwn Ddu of Mawddwy and Anna of Gwent, King Arthur's sister. Apprenticed at Illtyd (now Llantwit Major), Sampson began his missionary work in Cornwall, where he found a pagan tribe led by Gwedian. He converted them to Christianity, it is said, by bringing back to life a boy killed in a riding accident. Gwedian and his tribe, now convinced of Sampson's holy power, asked him to rid them of a troublesome serpent, which lived in a cave just half a mile (0.8 km) from Golant. After wading across the river, Sampson entered the serpent's dark lair and, invoking the name of Jesus Christ, killed the beast. He then instructed his followers to build a monastery, and continued his travels to Brittany. The present church, consecrated in 1509, is considered to occupy this site. The Trystan Stone, which now stands at 'Four Turnings', on the A3082, 1 mile (1.6km) to the north-west of Fowey, was taken from St. Sampson's. This sixth-century stone, inscribed 'DRUSTANUS HIC IACIT CUMOMORI FILIUS' (here lies Drustan [Trystan] son of Cunomorus), at one time marked the grave of Trystan, nephew of King Mark and lover of Mark's wife Queen Iseult. Mark was supposedly king of Cornwall during the sixth century, and had his palace at Lantyan, 2 miles north of Golant. History and legend have, however, become entwined, and there are some doubts about the authenticity of this.

Over

0   1 mile

0   1 km

1 *From Lostwithiel take the A390 to St. Austell. After about 1.5 miles (2.4 km), turn left on the B3269 towards Fowey. Then, after 3 miles (4.8 km), turn left at Castledore, following signs for Golant. When St. Sampson's church appears on a bend, you will see a wide layby on the right. Park here.*
From the church, walk downhill to Golant. Turn left at the crossroads by a chapel, and walk down to the tidal harbour. Walk alongside the harbour and turn right by the Fisherman's Arms.

6 *After about 600 yards (550 m), turn right at a stile indicated by a yellow Saints Way waymark. Walk across the field to a stile on the far right hand side. Cross it. Walk with a hedge on your left to cross another stile. Cross the lane, cross another stile, and walk across the field to a gate in the top right hand corner. Go through and walk to a stile half way along the right hand edge of the field. Cross it and walk ahead to join a hedge on your left. Turn left through a gate to return to the church.*

5 *When the track joins a tarmac surfaced lane, turn left to reach a crossroads. Go ahead along a lane to the left of the entrance to the Youth Hostel driveway.*

4 *Turn right and go through a gate marked Lanheriot Farm. Follow the lane to the farm. In front of the farm, follow the Public Footpath sign to walk along a rough track.*

3 *The path descends around Bodmin Pill and crosses a small stream on stones. Turn right immediately after the stream at a wooden post, and walk uphill through trees. When the path forks, go to the left, uphill. As you leave the trees, follow the path to the left of a hedgerow ahead. Continue with the hedgerow on your right. Go through two gates to join a road by some sheds.*

2 *Turn left at the T junction. By a pink house the road ends. Continue straight ahead along the path.*

CARN MARTH

4 miles (6.4 km) Moderate

0 ————————————————————————— 1 mile

0 ————————————————————————— 1 km

The view from Carn Marth encompasses the very oldest and one of the most famous mining areas in Great Britain. Tin has been extracted from around here for thousands of years. All the mines are gone now, although the Grambler engine-house can be seen in the direction of St. Agnes Beacon. Gone, too, are the thousands who once walked these tracks to hear John Wesley preach at Gwennap Pit.

1 *Start from the British Rail station in Redruth, where many buses also stop. Cars can be parked nearby. Redruth is situated at the junction of the A30 and A393.*
Go right from the station and fork right past the Wesley Chapel (1826). Pass Sea View Terrace on your right.

3 *Continue along a hedged track, pass an open space on your right, then follow a hedge on your left to an enclosed track. Continue through a gate to take another gate beside a signpost. Turn left along a track.*

4 *Look for a gap in the wall on your right. Turn right through it to take a path running parallel to a wall 20 yards (18 m) on your left. Go ahead over a stile beside a gate and continue beside a hedge on your left. Go through a gap ahead into the next field and veer very slightly right across this to another stile beside a gate. Cross this to pass a house on your right and take a hedged track to a lane junction.*

5 *Go ahead up the lane signposted Gwennap Pit. Look for a signpost pointing towards this on your right, and turn right here, passing a chapel to view the Pit. Resume your former direction along the lane to pass the entrance to Cathedral Farm on your right. Go on past a track on your left.*

2 *Come to a junction and turn right up Trefusis Terrace. Reach a crossroads with a telephone box, and turn left up Raymond Road. Cross Sandy Lane to take a signposted path past Grambler Farm on your left.*

6 *Turn right up a track which climbs gradually between blackberry bushes. Go ahead at a crosstracks and maintain your direction at a second crosstracks. Pass a ruined cottage on your left, and turn right at the third crosstracks.*

8 *Pass above a quarry behind a fence on your right, then bear right along a walled track. Descend to a lane and turn left. Pass a walled track on your left. Turn left at a T junction, turn right at the next junction and reach Raymond Road on your left. Go left along it, back to the start.*

7 *Follow the track, which gradually ascends the hill, passing tracks and a lake on your left. Continue beside a well covered in heather and gorse on your right. Ignore a gate on your right and go ahead to an OS trig. point on Carn Marth.*

The Museum of Cornish Methodism here is open Tues – Thurs 10am - noon, or by appointment (tel. 0209 212104 or 820381).

A Gwennap Pit may have been formed by an old mine working collapsing. The founder of Methodism, John Wesley, first preached here in 1762 and found it so convenient that he was to return 17 more times, his last visit being in 1789. Gwennap Pit became known as the 'Cathedral of Methodism', prompting a nearby farm to be renamed 'Cathedral Farm'.

B The view embraces Redruth to the west, above which is Carn Brea, with its monument and castle. St. Agnes Beacon can be seen in the north-east, and St. Austell lies to the east.

NANCLEDRA

4 miles (6.4 km) Moderate

0 ————————————————————————— 1 mile
0 ————————————————— 1 km

This is a varied walk, offering fine views, moorland, woodland, an Iron Age hillfort and an old china clay works. In summer, look out for wood anemones, pink purslane, spotted orchids, foxgloves and mare's tail on the first half of this route. When you reach Castle-an-Dinas, the hillfort within which is Rogers' Tower, you can also look out for the ghost of Wild Harris, a local landowner said to haunt this bleak spot.

2 *Reach a crosstracks and cross a stile beside a gate to the right of a lane ahead. Walk with a hedge on your left and continue over another stile. Veer right across the next field to a wooden gate beside a cottage. Continue through the gap opposite this to pass the front of the cottage, Little Amalebrea, and cross the field with its central hedge on your left.*

1 *Start from the Post Office in the village of Nancledra, which is on the B3311 midway between St. Ives and Penzance. There is a car park behind the Post Office. The no 16 bus (between Penzance and St. Ives) stops here.*
Go left onto the main road and take the next turning on your right
(signposted Georgia, Amalveor and Embla). Go ahead 500 yards (450 m) to cross a bridge and bear left at a fork. Pass a house on your left called The Moors, then turn left up a footpath just after it. Walk uphill for 500 yards (450 m).

3 *Go ahead over a stile beside a gate to enter a wood. Walk beside a stream, then pass rhododendrons as the path curves left past Tredorwin and its brick chimney. Turn sharply right at a path junction and pass above the chimney. After a further 50 yards (45 m), fork left.*

4 *Pass an old engine house, ignore the first path on your right but turn right over a metal bar across a gap in the bank shortly after it. Walk beside a wall on your right, on the other side of which is a lake. Reach the foot of a mound ahead. Go through a gap on your right to follow a rough path overlooking the lake. Reach some ruins and continue across a track to follow the uphill path between two posts with a hedge on your right. Cross the low wall at the top to bear left along a gravel track until another track goes left to a derelict farmhouse.*

7 *Turn right through a wooden gate. Cross a field, go through an iron gate and cross the next field to a small gate beside a field gate. Go ahead past a trough, through two more small gates beside field gates and down to a lane. Cross this to go down a narrow path back to the road. Go right to return to Nancledra.*

6 *Take a gap in the bank on your left to walk straight to Rogers' Tower. Go ahead, past it and the hillfort, to a small gap. Go through this and turn right along an old drove road. Follow this for 500 yards (450 m) to a metal gate ahead. Take a gap in the bank on your left just before this and continue beside the bank on your right. Reach a track and go left.*

5 *Bear left to the house, then turn right along a grassy track with a fine view of St. Michael's Mount ahead. A quarry is on your right.*

A This chimney was part of a china clay works, located here in the early 19th century. The china clay was taken by horse and cart to Penzance, then by ship to Liverpool for transport by canal to the Staffordshire potteries.

B The old engine house was used to pump water from the clay pit, which is now a lake.

C This is a mound of waste sand from the china clay works.

D Rogers' Tower was built as a folly in 1798.

23

MEN-AN-TOL

4.5 miles (7.2 km) Easy

There are prehistoric monuments to entice you on to this walk, and everyone will enjoy the view across Mount's Bay on a fine day. Ding Dong mine is of interest to industrial archaeologists, and the paths across the heather are bracing in all seasons.

A Men-an-Tol Studio is usually open for visitors to see exhibitions of etchings, linoprints, collographs and wood engravings. You can check by telephoning (0736) 68282.

B The Men-an-Tol monument is famous for its holed stone, indeed the name means Hole Stone in Cornish. The circular stone set on its edge with the hole through it is on a line between two upright stones, while a fourth stone lies fallen to the north-west of it. A plan drawn by Dr Borlase in the mid 18th century shows the western upright stone out of line, close to the fallen stone. This plan is believed to be inaccurate. The Victorian astronomer and scientist Sir Norman Lockyer may therefore be justified in claiming that the monument is aligned on the position of sunrise at the beginning of May and August plus, in the opposite direction, sunset position in February and November, marking the Celtic quarter days. This monument may date from the Stone Age or, at least, the Bronze Age, making it up to 6000 years old. The prime function of the stone was magical, rather than astronomical. Holed stones are associated with healing, with the sick person being passed through them. Apparently, to do this, you should be naked and here at the correct phase of the moon.

Adults should go through the hole nine times, while 'scrofulous children' should be passed through three times, then pulled over the grass three times against the sun. Apart from tuberculosis, the stones supposedly also cured lumbago, sciatica and infertility. They also ensured an easy childbirth and provided babies with a baptism of good health. Holed stones were also used for divination, with brass pins being laid across the top edge. Answers to questions would be given by the pins mysteriously moving.

C Men Scyrfa means, in Cornish, the stone of writing. It is inscribed with the words 'Rialobrani Cunovali Fili' (the last word is now below ground). This means 'of the Royal Raven, son of the Glorious Prince'. This Latinised Celtic dates the inscription to about AD500. The standing stone is said to mark the grave and also reproduce the exact height (six feet or 1.8 m) of this fallen warrior, killed in battle near this spot.

D The Nine Maidens is a stone circle currently consisting of five upright stones: two badly leaning and three fallen. In the mid 18th century, Dr Borlase recorded 13 upright stones and six fallen ones. The original total may have been 21 or 22 stones, averaging 4 feet (1.2 m) in height, with the highest stone being over 6 feet (1.8 m). The stones were evenly spaced in an accurate circle of 24 yards (21.9 m). The circle may have already been redundant by about 1250 BC, as this is the date given to a now dug-out barrow that once encroached on the southern side.

E Ding Dong is an ancient tin mine, which in tradition is said to have been visited by Jesus when he came to Britain with his uncle, Joseph of Arimathea. Its heyday was in the early 19th century. It closed in 1878, due to cheap tin imported from Malaya.

F Lanyon Quoit is a classic example of this type of monument. It is also a highly-restored specimen which differs significantly from the known original. When Dr Borlase came here in the mid 18th century, it consisted of a capstone 19 feet (5.8 m) long supported by four stones tall enough to allow a man on horseback to pass under it. This fell during a violent storm in 1815, breaking one of its stone supports. The reason for its fall after standing for 6000 years, since the New Stone Age, was excavations by such as Dr Borlase. These weakened the structure by removing soil from around its uprights. Local people subscribed to have the capstone re-erected on the three remaining stones in 1824.

Over

0   1 mile

0   1 km

3 *Fork right as waymarked by a yellow arrow and pass a derelict cottage on your left. Reach a crosspaths at the Four Parish Stone, at the point where Zennor, Gulval, Madron and Morvah parishes meet. Go half-right, uphill. Reach the summit and go right, past a round barrow.*

4 *Go ahead to the Nine Maidens stone circle. Pass this on your left and soon veer right towards the old Ding Dong mine, the engine house of which is a prominent landmark. Your path lies ahead, passing the engine house on your right, so only divert along the track bearing right for a closer inspection of the recently restored building. Continue down a gravel track. There is a fine view of St. Michael's Mount on your left.*

2 *Look for a signposted stile on your right and cross it to follow the path to the Men-an-Tol holed stone. Retrace your steps over the stile to turn right and resume your former direction. After 400 yards (365 m), notice the Men Scryfa standing stone in the centre of a field on your left.*

To Morvah

Men Scryfa **C**

B Men-an-Tol

D Nine Maidens

227m

P

A

E

Lanyon Farm

Bosiliack

F Lanyon Quoit

1 *Start from the Men-an-Tol Studio housed in the former Bosullow Schoolhouse, on the road between Madron and Morvah, 4 miles (6.4 km) north-west of Penzance. Nearby, beside a telephone box, there is a lay-by where cars can be parked.*
Take the signposted path opposite the Studio.

6 *Turn sharply right along the road. Bend left with the road for 100 yards (90 m), then veer right over a stone stile and cross a field to another stone stile. Go ahead over a farm drive and through a gate (or over it, if it is wired up!). Descend to a stile in the corner ahead. Go* *over it to return to the road, where you bear right to resume your previous direction. Notice Lanyon Quoit (see note F) on your right as you follow this road back to Men-an-Tol Studio, which is on your left.*

To Madron

5 *The gravel track turns into a lane and joins a road about 1 mile (1.6 km) south of Ding Dong mine.*

Walk 15

POLDARK MINE

4.5 miles (7.2 km) Easy, but may be muddy

As you walk around the area in which the Poldark Mine stands, all is quiet, green, peaceful and beautiful. Old chimneys excite the imagination, but it is very hard to relate this to the harsh industrial landscape of the 19th century, when almost 1000 people earned their living here. This is an opportunity to combine an attractive walk with a visit to a Cornish tin mine.

A Poldark Mine was originally known as Wheal Roots, and was one of 29 mines in the vicinity of Wendron in the 19th century. It is now a tourist attraction.

There are three routes through the workings to choose from. One is for the elderly, another for families, and the third for the adventurous and fit. The disabled cannot be catered for, and no dogs are allowed. Wheal Roots dates from the 1720s, has five shafts and three levels. The only power came from waterwheels and horses, with the miners labouring long hours in the dark and the damp to extract the ore.

The Cornish mines were developed by adventurers working under the cost book system: the adventurers would provide cash during bad times, but then take the profits during the good. This prevented the working managers of the mines from making necessary long term investments. Shafts would become crooked, machinery would wear out, ventilation would remain poor and little would be done to find new reserves.

The miners might be 'tut' workers or 'tributors'. Tut workers agreed a price for the volume or weight of material removed. Out of this would be deducted the cost of the candles, dynamite and tools, as supplied to them by the owners. This led to many accidents through miners saving on their candlelight. Tributors were paid an agreed share of the mineral raised from their pitch, this share being bid for in an auction where the lowest bid won, thus leaving a larger share for the owners. Good ground yielding plenty of ore was subject to the lowest bids, as the miners knew they would receive a regular income. There was often a battle of wits between the tributors and the mine managers regarding their knowledge of the nature of the ground. The price of tin was outside their control, however, so the low prices of the 1870s resulted in near starvation and the emigration of many Cornish tin miners to places such as Australia.

While the men drove the shafts and dug the ore, their families worked on the surface. 'Bal Maidens' crushed the ore into fine sand with heavy hammers or water-powered stamps. The waste was then washed away with running water. Children would spread the ore on tables; stir it up and let running water wash away the sand and leave the heavier tin grains.

Amongst the relics on display in the museum is a child's wheelbarrow. This is not a toy, but a working-tool for an eight-year old. The harsh living conditions of the 19th-century miners is shown in the reconstructed Poldark Village. This includes a General Store which only accepted the mine-owner's copper coins. Some of the costumes on display were used in the 1980s BBC TV series, Poldark.

The surface exhibits include the Greensplat Engine. This rotative beam engine worked at the Bunny tin mine in about 1850, then pumped clay slurry at Greensplat china clay pit from 1894 to 1959. A twin cylinder hoisting engine built by Holman Bros in 1905 is also on display. Open daily Apr - Oct, 10am - 6pm. Admission charge.

B St. Wendrona's church has a sixth-century Celtic cross near its south door.

Over

POLDARK MINE

Continued

1 Start from the Poldark Mine near the hamlet of Wendron, just off the B3297 2 miles (3.2 km) north of Helston. Cars can be parked here. Bus nos 37 and 39 (Helston to Truro) stop outside the mine. Cross the road from the mine entrance to take a track signposted 'Boderlogan Farm'.

2 Go between the farm buildings, then take the right-hand gate and walk with a hedge on your right to a gate in the top right field corner. This leads to a faint track which goes ahead down to a road, on the other side of which is a cottage.

3 Cross a stile to the left of the cottage and walk with a wall on your right to cross a second stile. Go ahead to cross a third stile, with a gate to its left. Keep the hedge on your right and go ahead through a gate. Bear half right down towards some cottages. Take a track on your left to the A394.

4 Turn right along the grassy verge of this main road for about 0.5 mile (0.8 km), passing two old mine chimneys on your left. When the road starts to dip, cross it with care and go left down from the road to a narrow, shady, track. This can be muddy, with a small stream running down it! It leads you to a lane.

5 Bear right along this lane to a road where you turn uphill. Bear right at a fork, away from Gweek. Go left at the next fork, uphill. Reach an S bend at the top of the hill. Look for a stile on your right, cross it to walk beside a hedge on your right. Turn right over a stile and turn left immediately to continue with the hedge now on your left. Go ahead to the A394.

6 Turn right to pass a telephone box on your left, then turn left along a signposted path. Ignore a turning to a farm on your left. Bear left at the next junction and turn right over a signposted stile at the next bend. Walk beside a wall on your right to a gate in the corner. Go ahead along a track and through a farmyard to reach a road.

7 Turn left for 20 yards (18 m) along the road, then turn right over a signposted stile to walk towards the tower of Wendron church. Go ahead over a stile in the corner and continue across a stile in the next. Go ahead to a kissing-gate across the road from the church. Continue along a track between the inn and the church. Go right at a junction to follow the churchyard wall to a kissing-gate. Go left beside a wall on your left to a stile. Cross this and a stile in the next corner to descend along a narrow path to a footbridge.

8 Climb up the narrow path to a track. Turn right along this to reach the B3297. Cross the road carefully and take the lane opposite, to return to the Poldark Mine, which is on your left.

0   1 mile

0   1 km

This is a gentle stroll past Falmouth Docks to Pendennis Point, where there are splendid views across to St Mawes (see Walk 17) and up the broad inlet called Carrick Roads to St. Just-in-Roseland. On the return, below Pendennis Castle, there are equally good views over Falmouth Bay to Pennance Point. **Please heed the warning notices regarding dangerous paths**.

1 *Start from Falmouth Quay station, the terminus for British Rail trains from Truro. There are buses to Falmouth from Penzance (2), Camborne (41 & 61) and Truro (69, 88 & 89). Motorists are advised to park in the large, free car park at The Hornworks and join the circuit at point 2. From the railway station, take the access road to a crossroads and go left, away from the railway bridge. Take the first turning on your left (Castle Drive). Follow it above the railway station and the docks on your left to reach the entrance to The Hornworks car park on your right.*

2 *Continue along the pavement of Castle Drive, with the sea on your left. Turn sharply right with the road at Pendennis Point and switch from the view across the mouth of the River Fal to St. Mawes to a view across Falmouth Bay to Pennance Point and, beyond, Rosemullion Head.*

4 *Fork right, downhill away from the sea. Either continue to the access road to the railway station, on your right, or turn right before that up Castle Drive if you need to return to the car park at The Hornworks.*

3 *Reach 'No Entry' signs (facing away from you) and turn sharply right up the drive to Pendennis Castle. Go back to the road and resume your former direction, with the sea on your left.*

A Falmouth has been an important port since the days of Sir Walter Raleigh. It provided shelter for ships awaiting favourable winds and was often the first place to replenish the supplies of vessels from across the Atlantic. Fast sailing-ships took letters and packets from here to America, Spain and Portugal. The existing docks were built in 1860, when Falmouth was the second busiest port in Britain, after London. The arrival of the railway in 1863 encouraged the growth of tourism.

B The Hornworks refers to an extension to Pendennis Castle. It was needed when Cromwell's army besieged the castle in 1646.

C Little Dennis Fort stands at sea level at the tip of the headland. It was probably built in the 1540s to provide auxiliary fire at sea level for Pendennis Castle, above it. Four guns were placed inside, while others were positioned on the roof. The battlements were designed to lessen the impact of shot by leaning inwards.

D Pendennis Castle was begun by King Henry VIII in 1540 and considerably added to by Queen Elizabeth I. Its purpose was to protect the deep, safe anchorage of the Fal estuary from use by enemy fleets. Gales prevented a second Spanish Armada from trying to take this strategic anchorage in 1597, but the castle saw noble action in 1646 when the Royalist Governor, Sir John Arundell, and 900 men, held out for five months against Sir Thomas Fairfax's Roundheads. It is open Easter – Sep daily 10am – 6pm and Oct – the day before Easter (exc. Christmas and New Year) Tues – Sun 10am – 4pm. Admission charge.

Walk 17
ST. JUST IN ROSELAND
6 miles (9.7 km) Easy

Stunning views across the estuary of the River Fal make this an exceptionally attractive walk. The outward route follows the coast alongside Carrick Roads, a ria, or drowned river valley. The return route, along a country road, keeps to the higher ground, giving splendid views in all directions.

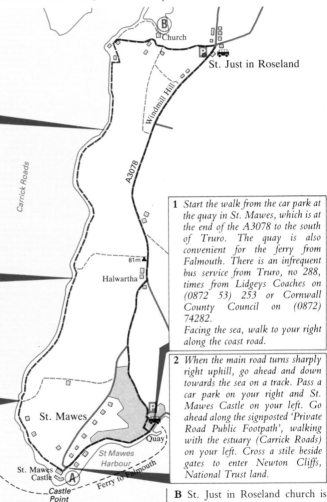

5 *Continue with the estuary on your left, and cross over two more stiles. Veer right inland near the end of the next field to cross a stile in the hedge ahead, above a bungalow on your left. Turn left after the bungalow to reach an access lane. Turn right along this and soon fork right. This lane leads past the church in St. Just. Turn right to walk carefully back along the road to St. Mawes.*

4 *Go over the stile ahead, then fork left at a signpost to descend beside a hedge on your left. Keep the estuary on your left and go over a stile ahead. Ignore a stile on your left in the next corner but cross a stile beside a gate. Follow the path over two more stiles beside gates, then over two more stiles before going down steps to cross a footbridge.*

3 *Ignore a signposted path on your right. Go ahead with the estuary on your left and through gaps into four more fields. Continue along a long, narrow field past woodland on your right. Ignore a stile on your left near this field's end.*

1 *Start the walk from the car park at the quay in St. Mawes, which is at the end of the A3078 to the south of Truro. The quay is also convenient for the ferry from Falmouth. There is an infrequent bus service from Truro, no 288, times from Lidgeys Coaches on (0872 53) 253 or Cornwall County Council on (0872) 74282.*
Facing the sea, walk to your right along the coast road.

2 *When the main road turns sharply right uphill, go ahead and down towards the sea on a track. Pass a car park on your right and St. Mawes Castle on your left. Go ahead along the signposted 'Private Road Public Footpath', walking with the estuary (Carrick Roads) on your left. Cross a stile beside gates to enter Newton Cliffs, National Trust land.*

A St. Mawes Castle is one of two coastal forts built by Henry VIII to defend the Fal estuary. Open daily 10am - 6pm (4pm in winter). Admission charge.

B St. Just in Roseland church is situated at the water's edge. Allow time to walk around the gardens and churchyard.

SANCREED

4 miles (6.4 km) Easy

Sancreed means holy faith in Cornish. If you have faith in holy well water, then you have a bonus on this route – not one but two to visit. This walk also takes you to a fogou, an ancient underground passageway, at the old beehive hut settlement of Carn Euny. The views, especially over to St. Michael's Mount, are grand. The gradient is never steep, with a succession of fields and stiles, plus some good tracks. Two early crosses stand by the church.

A Sancreed's church may have been founded by St. Credan, a late sixth-century Irishman. He was said to have earned his sainthood after abandoning the world in remorse having killed his father. The two crosses in the churchyard were most probably erected after his time, perhaps belonging to the eighth century. The taller one (at 9 feet, 2.7 m) by the diagonal path from the porch going south-east, is a fine example of incised work. One side shows Jesus above a lily, which may symbolise the Virgin Mary. There is some Latin lettering to suggest that this is an even older, re-used gravestone. The second cross is on the east side of the south porch. Jesus is on the front, complete with a halo, while another panel shows a serpent. The top of this cross used to stand on the churchyard wall. Its decorative shaft was found during restoration work in 1881 and it was re-erected in 1894.

B Sancreed's holy well is enchanting. You have to descend a flight of seven steps to the well, which is covered by a stone roof allowing ample headroom. As the entrance faces due south, the sun shines on the water at noon. It is a very peaceful spot with a reputation for making people sleep. The water is said to cure shingles, skin diseases, and to protect against witchcraft.

C Brane Cross stands on an old estate boundary, on a line from Boskawen-un stone circle to Boskenna Gate. Decorated with simple Latin crosses, it stands nearly 6 feet (1.8 m) high.

D The hillfort of Caer Bran was much more impressive before its thick stone walls were carted away for building in the 19th century. The site was probably connected with the local tin and copper trade which was flourishing in this area before the Romans came.

E Chapel Euny Holy Well is actually two dammed off parts of a stream which runs down to Lamorna Cove. Euny or Uny was an abbot who came to Cornwall from Ireland in the fifth century. The well is probably much older. When the archaeologist Dr Borlase visited it in the mid 18th century, he came upon two women bathing a child. They assured him that the only days to receive benefit from such a ceremony were the first three Wednesdays in May. Crippled, diseased and maimed children would then be dipped three times in the well against the stream of the running water.

F Carn Euny Fogou is the most interesting feature of an Iron Age village, probably dating from 400 BC, when the inhabitants lived in round huts built with timber over clay floors and stone covered drainage channels. This fogou is an underground passage of some 40 feet (12 m) in length, with a little side passage. Massive granite slabs covered with earth form the roof. Both ends are open and it is possible to walk through. The two ends of the main passage were originally blocked by stones, leaving the little side passage, which rose sharply to ground-level, as the only way in. As there is also a grain storage pit in the village, the usual claim that mysterious fogous were used to store food is not convincing. Neither was it a hiding place, with its roof and upper course well clear of the ground. The fogou has been dated to about 320 BC.

Over

0   1 mile

0   1 km

1 *Sancreed can be found by turning right off the A30, 2 miles (3.2 km) west of Penzance at Lower Drift. Start the walk from the Beacon Estate. This is where the no 9 bus stops (Hoppa from Penzance, Thurs & Fri only) and cars may be parked.*
Go down towards the church and bear right. Reach a junction and descend to the church on your left.

4 *Walk with a hedge on your right and maintain this direction over six more stiles. The sixth stile gives access to a track, but first notice Brane Stone Cross to the left of a stile opposite. You will return over this stile. Meanwhile, turn right and keep to this track, ignoring a left turn and easily avoiding dangerous old mineshafts. Reach Caer Bran, an old hillfort, and go ahead, bending right then left.*

5 *Turn left along a farm track. Ignore all turnings. The track narrows, then joins a T junction. Turn left and soon pass a house on your right. Follow the track as it bends left, then turn right along a path to reach Chapel Euny Holy Well. Go back to the main track and turn right to continue in the same direction as before for 50 yards (45 m). Turn left along a signposted path to Carn Euny Ancient Monument.*

6 *Leave Carn Euny by the bottom end, crossing a stile near the English Heritage noticeboards. Go ahead beside a hedge on your left to cross a field to a very broad track. Turn right along this to pass a car park, then turn left to pass some houses. Follow the road into Brane.*

7 *Reach a T junction at a white-painted house. Turn left and pass farm buildings. The road becomes a walled, grassy track. Go ahead through a gate and walk with a hedge on your left to a stile. Go over this and across the next field to another stile beside a gate. A hedge on your left points you in the right direction to cross the next field, but do not go through the metal gate. Instead cross the stile a little to its right. This is beside Brane Cross and you go ahead over the track to retrace your steps over the stile opposite to your starting point, with a fine view of Mount's Bay ahead.*

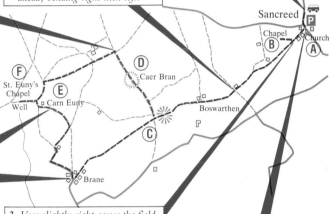

3 *Veer slightly right across the field, aiming for a solitary tree, and soon picking up a wall on your left. Go ahead over a stile, and with a wall now on your right, cut across the corner of a field to cross a stile on your right. Continue across the next field to a stile beside a gate, go over it and turn left down an old green lane. Keep beside a hedge on your right to cross another stile beside a gate in the corner ahead. Continue across a track and past a shed on your right to follow a narrow path to a field.*

2 *Cross the road from the church to a telephone box and take a signposted path to the holy well. This path goes through a small gate, over a yard and across a stile beside a gate to the right of a building. Go ahead towards another stile, but do not cross it yet. Instead, divert to the right along the narrow, signposted path to Sancreed well. This passes low buildings on your left before crossing a stile to go between trees to the well and chapel, near which is a modern cross. Retrace your steps to the main path and resume your former direction by crossing the stile on your right.*

Walk 19
MERRY MAIDENS
4.5 miles (7.2 km) Easy

This route introduces you to the glory of inland Cornwall, especially to the standing stones which characterise West Penwith.

Ancient paths using stone stiles to cross old boundary walls lead to the best preserved stone circle in Cornwall. There is a wealth of neighbouring monuments, and it is not far from the start of the walk to Lamorna Cove, from where the Coastal Path leads to Mousehole.

A The standing stone across the hedge is one of a pair. Rising nearly 9 feet (2.7 m) out of the ground, it is aligned with the south-west Piper stone and the Merry Maidens stone circle a little over half a mile (0.8 km) to the north-east. Its 7.5 foot (2.3 m) companion lies in the hedge to the west, having been moved earlier this century. In fact, both stones were uprooted but this one was reinstated when it was found preferable to have it as a rubbing-stone for cattle, rather than have the cattle knocking down the hedgerows.

B Wayside crosses indicated the routes for travellers across Cornwall in bygone days. They aren't necessarily Christian in origin. The cross was an important spiritual symbol long before Jesus became known to the druids (as Cornish tradition states). They seem to have had a phallic purpose in the marriage between earthly and cosmic forces. This particular one is decorated with the figure of Jesus, and may have been carved a thousand years ago, long after the stone was originally erected. It now stands at the side of the road, where it was moved to prevent damage from passing army lorries during World War II. Originally it would have stood in the middle of the road, aligned with the Merry Maidens stone circle and another cross to the west.

C Choone Cross has lost its shaft, since its base is out of proportion. A figure of Jesus has been carved on the cross.

D This magnificent 10.5 foot (3.2 m) high standing stone is called Gun Rith, meaning Red Downs. Its bulbous head is thought by many to give it a phallic significance, perhaps connected with the May Day fertility festival of Beltane.

E It is worth making the short diversion down the road to see the Tregiffian Barrow, although it was mutilated by construction of the road in 1840. When excavated in the 1960s, a cupmarked stone was found and taken away to the County Museum in Truro. It was replaced by a concrete replica. The cupmarks amounted to 12 oval and 13 circular, which may refer to the number of full moons and new moons in a year. Cremated remains and an undamaged urn were also found here.

F The Merry Maidens is one of the best preserved stone circles in Britain. Its 19 stones include only three that had to be re-erected in the 19th century, and they are equally spaced with an entrance gap on the eastern side, where there may have been a processional way. The view from the circle of the twin hills Chapel Carn Brea and Bartinney has a resemblance to the breasts of the Earth Goddess. The dowser Tom Lethbridge dated the circle to 2540 BC, which was later confirmed by archaeologists. The Cornish name for the stones is *Dans Men* or *Dawns Meyn*, which could refer to dancing or just to sacred stones. Maiden is a corruption of meyn or men, meaning stone (and pronounced main in Cornish). Merry is derived from Mary or Mari, the fertile mother worshipped as a goddess in the Middle East in 1000 BC. The legend is that some merry maidens were turned to stone for dancing here on a Sabbath. The two Pipers who played the music were also turned into stones (see **G**).

G These two standing stones are known as the Pipers – they who played the tunes for the merry maidens to dance to. They are 15 feet (4.5 m) high.

Over

0   1 mile

0   1 km

5 Follow the hedge on your left to a stile in the corner and cross it to reach a road. Notice Boskenna Cross on your left, then cross the road to take the road to St. Buryan. Look for another cross on your right, just before some cottages. This is Choone Cross. Retrace your steps 80 yards (72 m) and cross a stile beside a gate now on your left. Go towards the right of a house below. Cross a stile, cross the drive and then another stile. Then bear half-left through a gap in an old wall to pass a gated corner on your right. Go left parallel to a hedge on your right until you go right over a stile 150 yards (135 m) before a corner.

6 Cut across the field to a stile. Go over it, and an overgrown lane, to a stile on the right opposite. Turn right to a gap in the corner with a standing stone. Bear left to reach a road. Tregiffian Barrow is on your right, but continue over a stile ahead to the stone circle. Leave this field by a stile on your left in the top right corner. Go ahead, bearing right to a stile beside a telephone pole. Emerge at a bend in a road and veer right up an access lane towards Menwinnion Country House. Continue down an old green lane back to the road in the Lamorna Valley. Turn right to walk back to the start.

1 Start from the Post Office at Lamorna, which is on your left as you approach Lamorna Cove, near the junction of a lane from Mousehole via Castallack with the road down Lamorna Valley, about 4 miles (6.4 km) south of Penzance. Cars may be parked considerably at the roadside nearby, and the 316 bus from Penzance stops here.
Go up the lane opposite, signposted to Lamorna Hotel. Pass the hotel on your left. Continue to a sharp right turn and go right to pass a house called Tregurnow Cliff. Bear left through a metal gate and along a hedged track.

The Pipers

Ⓒ Ⓖ

Ⓓ Ⓔ Merry Lamorna
Maidens

B3315 Ⓕ

Ⓑ Boskenna Cross

Lamorna Valley

Ⓐ

Rosemodress

Boscawen
Rose

4 Cross the farmyard, with the right of way using a big stone stile. Go through a gateway on the right to reach a corner of a field. Ignoring a gate ahead, veer left to the corner of a hedge jutting out into a field on your left. Go ahead with this hedge on your right almost to the far corner, then, cross the field to a stile on your left. Go over it and follow a hedge on your left, noticing a standing stone in the field on its other side. Cross a stile in the field corner ahead and veer very slightly right across the next field and over a stile in the hedge opposite. Cut across a field to join a hedge on your left.

3 Go ahead to a broken step stile in a wall beside a cottage on your right. Cross this and turn right along a lane, passing a farm on your right and around a bend to your left, then to your right. Just after this bend, turn left over a stile in the hedge. Walk with a hedge on your left to a track and turn right along it to a farm. Pass the farmhouse on your right. Then, just before the last buildings on your left, turn left.

2 Cross a stile beside a gate and bear right past a farm. Turn left over a stile. Continue with a hedge on your left to a step stile in it just after a bend. Cross this and go half right to a stile in the wall beside a telephone pole. Go over this to walk beside a hedge on your right to a stile in the field corner ahead. Bear right to a gateway and go left past buildings. Pass one signpost, then go ahead through a gate beside another signpost and an electricity pole. Continue beside a hedge on your right and over a stile ahead.

Walk 20
GWEEK
5 miles (8 km) Easy, but can be muddy in places

This route starts by following one of the streams which feed the head of the Helford Estuary. It then goes across country, with some splendid views, to return to Gweek near a second stream which feeds the Helford. There is plenty of variety, with the welcome presence of trees, but no really steep hills. Allow time to visit the Seal Sanctuary.

A Pollard Mill has been attractively restored. Its wheel is in good condition and its leat (water supply channel) is kept clear from here to the bridge over the road.

B Here you can see the sluice-gate which enables the stream water to be channelled into the leat for Pollard Mill.

C When you reach Boskenwyn Manor, look back for a splendid view over to the Goonhilly Satellite Earth Station. Work started on it in 1961 and the first live television picture from America was received with the aid of the Telstar satellite on 11th July, 1962. The honour of receiving this first transatlantic signal was shared with a similar station in Brittany. The first Goonhilly aerial was about 90 feet (27 m) in diameter and weighed 1100 tons. There are now 10 aerials here. Some are relatively small, but one has a diameter of nearly 100 feet (30 m) and is called 'Blue Peter' after the children's television programme that featured its opening in the early 1980s. You can visit the station to learn all about the tens of millions of messages that go through Goonhilly each year. These include telephone calls, data and facsimile transmissions as well as television and radio signals. Visitors can also enjoy an audio-visual show in the museum, a shop, a restaurant and a guided tour of the site by bus. Open Easter - Oct daily 10am - 6pm. Admission charge.

D Tol-ven means Holed Stone in Cornish. Like Men-an-Tol (Walk **14**), this stone has a reputation for healing. A Victorian recorded the practice of passing a sick child through the hole nine times. The child would then sleep on a mound nearby with a sixpence under its head. Some believe that the hole was caused naturally by weathering. Others suggest that it may have been cut. Holed stones occur in other parts of the British Isles, including Ireland and Orkney. The smaller stones were moved to where they were needed, while others were soaked in a liquid which was then taken to the patient.

E Gweek used to be an important port. The Phoenician tin traders probably came here, and the Romans built forts nearby, just to the north of Boskenwyn and to the east of Tolvan. This was for centuries the port of Helston, which was a prosperous borough in the 13th century and a tin coinage town, like Truro, Lostwithiel and Launceston. Access to its own quays was closed off by the advancing sands of the Loe Bar, making Gweek the natural port for Helston. By 1201, Gweek had its own merchant guild and burgess privileges. The mining that brought the commerce also deposited waste material in the streams and silted up the River Helford. Cargo ships still made it up here in the 1930s, and Truro river barges called here regularly until 1945. Charles Kingsley set the Cornish adventures of his novel *Hereward the Wake* (published in 1866) here.

F When miner Ken Jones took early retirement, he moved with his wife to Cornwall, rescued a seal and went on to create this sanctuary, complete with a special hospital. His story is related in the book *Seal Doctor*. An exhibition centre with audio-visual shows will tell you about the origins and work of the Seal Sanctuary – and give information about the sea-mammals of the world. The hospital has pens and two small pools where injured or abandoned seal pups are cared for. The winter is the best time to see them. There are always seals in the 10 sea pools, including maternity, nursing, weaning and resident pools. The Sanctuary is open Oct - Easter daily (except Christmas) 9.30am - 6pm. Feeding times are at 11am and 4pm.

Over

0   1 mile

0   1 km

4 *Go through the farmyard and fork left to pass the house and barn on your right. Go ahead through a gate and veer slightly right across a field to a stile beside a gate to the right of electricity supply poles. Cross the stile and continue beside a hedge on your left. Reach Boskenwyn Manor.*

5 *Turn right along a track to a road. Go right. Pass a school on your left and, at a junction, go ahead towards Gweek. Ignore a right fork, then an entrance to Barton Farm on your left. Pass Trenoweth on your left. Just after passing Boskenwyn chapel on your right, cross the road with care to take a hedged track on your left. Descend to a stream.*

6 *Cross the stone slab bridge. Bear right uphill to a road. Notice the Tol-ven stone in the back garden of a house on your left. Turn right down the road back to Gweek. Go ahead up the lane signposted 'Cornish Seal Sanctuary'. Retrace your steps to the B3291 in Gweek and turn left to go over the bridge back to the bus shelter.*

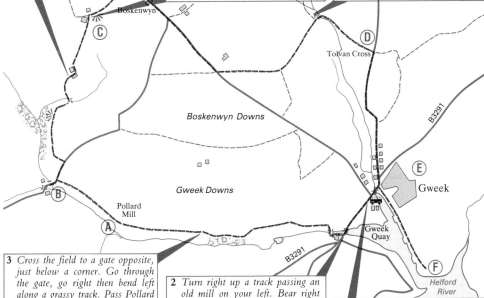

3 *Cross the field to a gate opposite, just below a corner. Go through the gate, go right then bend left along a grassy track. Pass Pollard Mill and follow its drive to a road. This route continues to the right, uphill along the road, but first divert to your left to see the sluice gate for the mill leat from the bridge. Back on the uphill road, take a concrete track (and cross a cattle grid) on your left to Pollard Farm. Walk with a hedge on your right and a view of a beautiful wooded valley on your left.*

2 *Turn right up a track passing an old mill on your left. Bear right over a bridge across a stream and follow a shady track as it bends left. Pass the last house on your left and go ahead over a stile beside a gate. Continue beside a hedge on your right and through two gates. Veer left to the bottom of the next field and walk with woodland on your left to go through a gate in the corner ahead. Continue just inside the hedge on your left to the corner of the field and veer left to a kissing-gate. Go through this.*

1 *Gweek is about 3 miles (4.8 km) east of Helston, on the B3291. Start from the bus stop at Gweek Quay. This is served by nos 294 (Truro to Mawgan), 299 (Helston to Falmouth), 311 & 313 (Helston to St. Keverne) and 312 (Helston to Constantine). Cars can be parked considerably at the roadside nearby.*
With your back to the bus shelter, go left towards Helston. Go ahead over a bridge.

Walk 21

ST. MARY'S – ISLES OF SCILLY

5.5 miles (8.9 km) Easy

The Isles of Scilly are the ideal venue for a day trip and, of course, a longer stay. The roads are narrow, quite charming and virtually free of traffic. Paths are good and well used, and there is much to see, and no better way to see it than on foot. The three main transport routes are as follows, in ascending order of cost.

By sea The passenger ferry *Scillonian III* sails from Penzance to St. Mary's, the voyage taking 2½ hours. Details from the Isles of Scilly Steamship Co., Quay Street, Penzance, Cornwall TR18 4BD. Tel. Penzance (0736) 62009.

By aeroplane Two ten seater Islander aircraft operate from Land's End Aerodrome to St. Mary's, the flight taking 15 minutes. Details from Isles of Scilly Skybus, Land's End Aerodrome, St. Just, Penzance, Cornwall TR19 7RL. Tel. Penzance (0736) 787017. You must book in advance.

By helicopter 32 seater Sikorsky S61N's fly from Penzance Heliport to St. Mary's and Tresco, the flights taking 20 minutes. Details from British International Helicopters, The Heliport, Penzance TR18 3AP. Tel. Penzance (0736) 63871 (late bookings 64296). You must book in advance.

A bus meets all incoming and outgoing flights and terminates in a square known as The Bank, in Hugh Town, where the walk starts. This is just around the corner from The Mermaid Inn, which is right by the harbour where the Scillonian III docks. The route goes around the northern side of St. Mary's, where most of the 'off islands' – Samson, Bryher, Tresco and St. Martin's – can be seen. It then crosses the centre, where sub-tropical plants thrive in the shelter of the land.

A Harry's Walls are the scant remains of a 17th-century fortification, offering a fine panoramic view. The windmill-like structure is a navigational mark for shipping.

B Telegraph Tower is the old Coastguard tower, built at 160 ft (50 m) on the highest point of the island. It is where the daily 'reports from coastal stations' for the Scillies comes from, on the BBC shipping forecast.

C Halangy Village was a settlement re-established in 200 BC on the site of an earlier village occupied in 1500 BC by the builders of Bant's Carn burial chamber, which can be seen further up the hill. The village remained in use for several centuries.

D There is a splendid view across to Tresco from here. It is the second largest island in the group, and widely known for its Abbey Gardens, an exotic sub-tropical garden created in 1834 by Augustus Smith.

E There are two burial chambers at Innisidgen, both of which are in an excellent state of repair. Also serving as shrines or temples, they were built 2000-1500 BC at a time when the Isles of Scilly formed one large island.

F To the north is St. Martin's Island. Between this and Tresco is Tean, which was cultivated until 1822, and a great many smaller islands and rocks. It is easy to understand why there have been so many shipwrecks around the islands.

G Holy Vale is thought to have been the site of a monastic cell – now it is a tiny settlement with very exotic gardens. The Nature Trail starts here and passes through a moist valley of elm and wych-elm, unique on the island. During the spring and early summer the ground is carpeted with bluebells and wild garlic, and the trees attract woodland species such as warblers and flycatchers, a contrast to the seabirds which predominate on the Scillies.

Over

0   1 mile

0   1 km

4 *The track forks. Go to the left, following the sign to 'Innisidgen Burial Chambers'. Pass the first chamber and continue until another sign directs you to the second, where the path again forks, and you go to the left and continue along the path to Watermill Cove.*

5 *Go down the steps and head inland along the path, which joins a track. Maintain your direction until the track joins a tarmac road, where you turn left. Turn left at a small green by a post box, then after 100 yds (90 m), turn sharp right by a palm tree, following a sign to the Longstone Heritage Centre.*

3 *Cross the stile and turn left onto a track, which soon splits into four. Go straight ahead taking the track immediately to the right of the two gateposts which are the entrance to Gorse Cottage. The track at first curves around to the right, and then gently to the left above a rocky beach. When it joins another track, turn sharp left to once again walk with the sea to your left. After about 100 yds (90 m) the track splits. Take the right fork and continue.*

2 *Follow the road, keeping the sea to your left. After 300 yards (275 m) the road turns sharp right. A path, signposted 'To Juliets Garden', continues ahead. Take this path and follow it around the coast, passing Halangy Village and eventually coming to a green metal gate with a stile beside it.*

1 *From The Bank square, walk away from the harbour, forking left when you pass the Bishop & Wolf pub on your right, and keeping the sea to your left. Shortly after passing the comprehensive school on your right, look out for a path to your left, signposted 'To Harry's Walls, 16th century fort'. Follow the sign, taking what is the start of the coastal path. After 300 yards (275 m) you pass below the fort, which is signposted to your right. If you visit the ruins, make sure that you rejoin the path, which continues past some houses to join a road.*

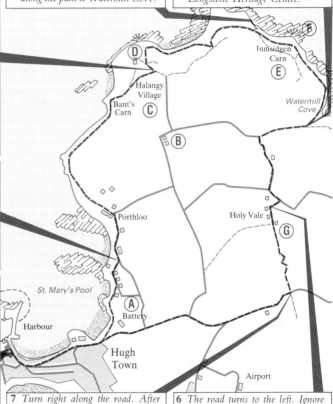

7 *Turn right along the road. After 600 yds (550 m), ignore a left fork and continue to a T junction. Turn left here to walk back to The Bank.*

6 *The road turns to the left. Ignore further signs to the Longstone Heritage Centre, but continue ahead passing a house and Middle Tinks cottage, to join the 'Holy Vale Nature Trail'. Follow the trail to a road.*

Part of this walk follows a section of The North Devon Coast Path. This is very demanding, but provides splendid views. If it is a clear day, you should see Lundy and South Wales. You can also visit one of the delightful beaches just below the path. As these are only accessible to walkers they are often deserted. The inland return is an attractive, peaceful path past a standing stone.

2 *Turn right along the Coast Path to walk above the sea on your left. Go over a stile in a wall and note an optional diversion down to Rockham Beach on your left. Continue over a stile beside a gate to enter National Trust land at Bull Point. Follow the signposted path at first right, then left, through a gap in a wall.*

3 *Continue along the Coast Path to pass the lighthouse at Bull Point on your left, but ignoring the access road going inland to your right. Go down steps to a stile before a footbridge. Cross these to zigzag uphill (on the National Trust's Damage Cliffs) to a stile at the top. Go ahead across it.*

4 *With the sea still on your left, descend to cross another footbridge. Ignore a stile on your left (leading down to a cove). Climb steps with a fence on your left, then go down steps to a gate to reach a lane. Go right, inland, along this for about 350 yards (320 m).*

5 *When the lane bends left, go to the right along a signposted and hedged path. Continue over a stile beside a gate to take a fenced track. Cross a stile beside a gate and turn right at a track junction through the higher of two gates. Go ahead beside a fence on your right.*

6 *Just before the track bends right, turn left over a stile in the fence and walk parallel to a fence on your left. Pass a standing stone in the middle of the field on your right. Continue over a stile in the bottom corner, go ahead over a footbridge and turn left up a path which climbs to a lane. Turn left along this lane back to Mortehoe.*

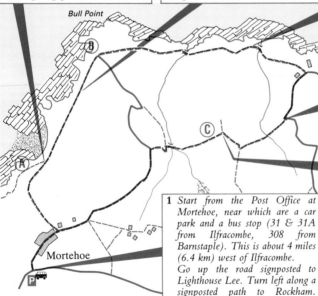

1 *Start from the Post Office at Mortehoe, near which are a car park and a bus stop (31 & 31A from Ilfracombe, 308 from Barnstaple). This is about 4 miles (6.4 km) west of Ilfracombe. Go up the road signposted to Lighthouse Lee. Turn left along a signposted path to Rockham. Descend to the Coast Path.*

A The North Devon Coast Path is part of the South West Way, which runs for over 570 miles from Minehead to Poole. You will often see weary backpackers along this path!

B There has been a lighthouse at Bull Point since 1879. This one replaced the original, which was made unsafe by rock falls in 1972.

C The ancient standing stone in the middle of the field has no doubt survived because it is useful as a cattle-rub. It served an unknown purpose in the dim and distant past.

MORTE POINT

2.5 miles (4 km) Moderate

The National Trust owns the stretch of coastline which the initial part of this route follows. These low cliffs are not ideal places for sea-birds, but look out for rock pipit and wheatear. In clear weather you will enjoy fine views, including Lundy island to the west, before you go inland for the return to Mortehoe, with its interesting parish church.

4 *Ignore a second narrow path forking right, pass a second bench on your right, and zigzag uphill. Pass two seats overlooking Rockham Bay, ignore a third path on your right but go ahead just 20 yards (18 m) more.*

5 *Fork right inland beside an old wall on your left. Reach a wall on your right, but ignore the stile and the gate in it. Go ahead through a kissing-gate and along a track to pass a cemetery on your right. Go left along a lane back to Mortehoe.*

6 *Pass the church on your right and go left back to the start.*

1 *Start from the Post Office at Mortehoe, near which are a car park and a bus stop (31 & 31A from Ilfracombe, 308 from Barnstaple). This is about 4 miles (6.4 km) west of Ilfracombe. Go down the road towards Woolacombe, passing the parish church on your right. Ignore a signposted path on your right before a Methodist church.*

3 *Follow the Coast Path. Go ahead over a stile and around Morte Point. Ignore the first path on your right after the point. Pass a bench on your right and enjoy the view of Rockham Bay ahead.*

2 *Leave the road by taking a gate on your right to enter National Trust land at Morte Point. Go down the path to join the Coast Path. Turn right along this to walk with the sea on your left.*

A Morte Stone extends into the sea beyond the tip of Morte Point. It is a treacherous spot and five ships were wrecked on it in the winter of 1852. This prompted the construction of a lighthouse at nearby Bull Point (Walk **22**). According to legend, Morte Stone may be moved by any man who is master of his wife. Needless to say, it is still in place. The tip of Morte Point was used as a target for bombing practice in World War II. Come in August or September to see the heather, amidst which gorse stands like yellow islands in a purple sea, and watch out for fulmars, stonechats and white throats.

B St. Mary's is the parish church of Mortehoe. The Normans seem to have built the first little chapel here, but open-air services were probably held on the site as far back as the days of the Celtic St. Brannock, who came from Wales in the sixth century. Although only a hamlet, Mortehoe was already recorded as a parish in 909 when the diocese of Crediton was created. By 1270, the church had a strong tower. Sir William Tracy is recorded as founding the Chantry of St. Mary Magdalene and St. Catherine in 1307. He is now buried in it. It is a possibility that his ancestor, an earlier Sir William de Tracy, is buried with him. He was one of the murderers of Thomas à Becket, the Archbishop of Canterbury, in 1170. Tradition states that he lived in Mortehoe before confessing his crime. The impressive mosaic over the chancel arch is modern.

Walk 24
STOKE
4 miles (6.4 km) Moderate

The parish of Hartland was once known as the place in all England farthest from railways. This is a corner of Devon where nature still seems to be in command, whether along the rugged cliffs or in the richly wooded valleys. The walk includes a fine array of water features: a mill; spectacular waterfalls; and a quayside; plus a visit to Hartland's parish church, which is actually located in Stoke.

A Docton Mill is an ancient mill, now restored. A richly wooded garden has also been created in this wild valley. It is only 1 mile (1.6 km) from the fierce Atlantic gales, but they roar overhead in this sheltered spot which nestles below a wooded hillside. The first watermill on this site was worked by the Saxons but no corn has been ground here since the last miller died in 1914. The water wheel has been restored, but now generates electricity to heat the mill house. The garden has been planned to blend with its surroundings. Over 1100 mixed broadleaved trees have been planted on a formerly open hillside. There is an abundance of wild woodland, wild flowers and ferns. As the shelter has been improved, the garden areas have been extended. The summer garden is in a sunny enclave behind a beech hedge. The wild stream is crossed by footbridges to the orchard and the waterfall garden, which features water splashing down from the mill pond. The orchard is a traditional feature, with apple wood being used to make the mill's hard-wearing equipment. The leat (water channel) bank above the orchard leads to the mill pond. A little stone bridge gives access to the mill garden and the wheel. Take the rising, cobbled path above the mill and the rockery to enter the bog and woodlands garden. Go even higher along the badger walk for a superb view across the valley. Open Sun – Thurs Apr – Sept 10am – 5pm. Admission charge.

B This waterfall is at Speke's Mill Mouth. Reckoned to be the best on the whole North Devon Coast Path, it falls over 50 feet (15 m) from a height of over 150 feet (45 m) above sea level, over one limb of a V shaped fold in the rocks. Then the water flows along a level trough for nearly 135 feet (40 m) before turning at a right angle to cut its way towards the sea through the ridge-shaped fold beyond, descending in three small falls. The stream here has cut a young gorge or canyon into the cliffs, and, in time, the floor of the gorge could be cut down to sea level. The big waterfall inland has been formed by the trough at its foot, and it is a good example of an almost sheer fall.

C The distinctive St. Catherine's Tor is said to have been surmounted by a Roman villa. Perhaps this was a chapel dedicated to the saint. Much of the tor has fallen into the sea since Roman times.

D Hartland Quay was petitioned for by the Great Elizabethan sailors Drake, Raleigh and Hawkins, when Hartland was bigger than Bideford. Its artificial harbour was swept away in 1896. As many as 35 shipwrecks were recorded near here between 1862 and 1904, including the Italian steamship, the *Rosalia*, 2000 tons, which was totally wrecked in very thick fog in Hartland Quay in 1904.

E The parish church of Hartland is dedicated to the fifth-century Celtic saint, Nectan. He arrived from Wales to lead a hermit's life. Apparently, on 17th June (now commemorated as his saint's day), in an unknown year, he was beheaded by some local bandits. He is then said to have walked to the holy well at Stoke and placed his head on a stone there before he died. His church wasn't built until 1055 by Gytha, the mother of the Harold who lost the Battle of Hastings. The present church dates from the 14th century and has the second highest tower in Devon, at 128 feet (39 m). St. Nectan's relics were preserved beneath the high altar until the Reformation. The rood screen is late 15th century.

F Hartland Abbey lies between Stoke and Hartland. It was built in 1160 and has been a family home since the Dissolution in 1539. It is open May – Sep Sun, Bank Holiday Mon & Wed 2 - 5.30pm. Admission charge.

Over

0   1 mile

0   1 km

6 *Hartland Quay is down on your left. This route continues by going right along the road, inland. Keep right at a fork and pass the Rocket Apparatus House on your left. Go*

ahead along the road back towards Stoke. Go over a stone stile in the wall of the churchyard to return to the start of the walk.

1 *Start from St. Nectan's church, which is in Stoke, 2 miles (3.2 km) west of Hartland. This is about 15 miles (24 km) west of Bideford. Cars may be parked considerately at the roadside nearby.*
Walk from the church back towards Hartland, passing the public toilets on your left, and very soon turn right up a lane. Go ahead at a crossroads along a rough lane signed 'unsuitable for motors'.

2 *Maintain your direction at the next crossroads, taking the lane ahead signposted to Elmscott and Welcombe.*

3 *Turn right at a crossroads just before a bridge (and near a letter box). This lane is signposted Docton Mill. Notice a track on your right signposted as a public footpath – you will return here to follow it. First proceed along the lane to a gate on your left which is signed as the mill entrance. After visiting the mill, return to the signposted track and turn left onto it. It soon bends left. The hedges on both sides disappear and the path climbs above the stream on your left.*

4 *Ignore a signposted path on your right. Go ahead towards the sea. Ignore a footbridge below on your left but, 100 yards (90 m) after it, notice a stream dropping over 50 feet (15 m), forming a spectacular waterfall to a trough leading to the sea.*

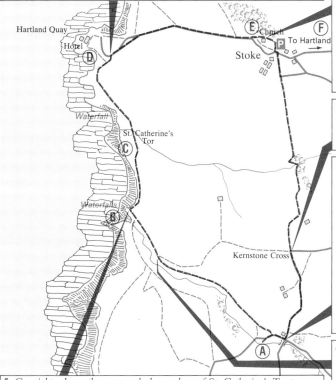

Hartland Quay

Hotel

D

Waterfall

St. Catherine's Tor

C

Waterfalls

B

E Church

P To Hartland

F

Stoke

Kernstone Cross

A

5 *Go right along the waymarked Coast Path above the sea on your left. Climb wooden steps over a wall and continue beside a fence overlooking the sea on your left. Bear right inland to a gate in the wall ahead. Go right around the*

base of St. Catherine's Tor to pass it on your left. Take the stepping-stones over a stream, cross a stile at the foot of the Tor, with a wall extending to its right. Continue with the Coast Path through a gate and up steps to a road.

Scale: 0 — 1 mile / 0 — 1 km

Clovelly is a picturesque estate village of unique character, overlooking magnificent coastal scenery and bounded by romantic woods with well laid out paths.

After following the Coast Path, you turn inland beside a stream, through the trees and across fields to a clear track back to the access road. The 'Angels' Wings', an unusual summer house, is passed on the walk. This would make an ideal place for a picnic.

3 Go left along the path waymarked with an acorn symbol and follow the Coast Path when it turns sharply right after 20 yards (18 m). Descend to Mouth Mill, and reach an old lime kiln. Turn left, inland. Ignore the signposted Coast Path on your right.

2 Ignore a signposted path to the church on your left. Bear right along the signposted Coast Path, passing the 'Angels' Wings' (an unusual summer house) on your right. Emerge from the trees at the top of Gallantry Bower, 350 feet (106 m) high, from where you may enjoy a view of Lundy. Ignore a path on your left as you descend through the trees.

1 Start from the Visitor Centre at Clovelly, where there is a car park (fee, including admission to the Centre). This is 1 mile (1.6 km) north of the A39, about 10 miles (16 km) west of Bideford. There is a bus stop here (B from Ilfracombe, 319 from Bideford). Walk to the left at the top signpost, with the sea on your right. Reach a Coast Path signpost where the road forks. Do not go downhill along the road on your right, but do take the waymarked gate just above it to your left. Go right to a Coast Path signpost where you bear right along the waymarked path, keeping the sea on your right. Continue through a kissing-gate, then take another in the fence on your right. Go ahead along the Coast Path.

Blackchurch Rock

Deer Park

B

Church

P

A

Clovelly

Clovelly Bay

4 Reach a T junction with a signposted bridleway. Go left and left again at a second signpost. Turn right up a woodland path at a third signpost. Emerge through a gate at the top to follow the forest fence on your left to a signposted gate in the corner. Go through this and veer right to a gate above the trees.

5 Go ahead along a track which becomes a lane and passes a church on your left. Turn left upon reaching a road and fork right back to the start. From here you can explore the village street.

century harbour and the panoramic coastal views. Clovelly is the estate village of the Hamlyn family, lords of the manor.

B All Saints church, Clovelly, houses a tablet to Will Cary of *Westward Ho!* fame. Charles Kingsley's father was rector here.

A Clovelly is an extraordinary picture postcard village which epitomises the West Country. If you are visiting the area, bring your camera to record the quaint village street, the restored 14th-

0   ·   1 mile

0   1 km

When land here was released to allow the construction of the railway in 1854, the local landowner made it a condition that all trains must stop at Eggesford, which has remained to this day a particularly tranquil spot. As it is about half way along a single track line, it has become a convenient passing place. Alight for forests, a fast-flowing river and rolling hills.

1 *Start from British Rail's station at Eggesford, on the Tarka Line from Exeter to Barnstaple. Motorists may park near the church at point 2 and start the circuit there. The church can be found by turning off the A377 beside the station, driving over the level crossing and taking the first left.*

Turn right from the station over the bridge across the River Taw. Pass an access drive, then a road on your right. Go ahead 100 yards (90 m), then turn left along the lane towards Eggesford Garden Centre. Pass the entrance to this on your right and go ahead to a church.

2 *Go ahead along the signposted track, passing the church on your left. Fork right at a waymark post to take the upper track almost to Eggesford Barton Farm. Look out for a sign on a telephone pole on your left. This points to a path on your right. Turn sharply right here up a grassy track which soon bears left, then right, to a gate in the top field corner.*

3 *Continue through the gate and beside a hedge on your left. Pass old barns on your left and an isolated stile on your right. Go ahead through a gate and follow the grassy track to reach a road by Eggesford Fourways, where there is a war memorial.*

4 *Turn right along the road for 350 yards (320m), then go to the left up a track, signposted as a public bridleway. Pass the entrance to Old Glebe on your left and pass a farmhouse on your right. Keep to the clearer track bearing right at a fork. Go ahead through a gate.*

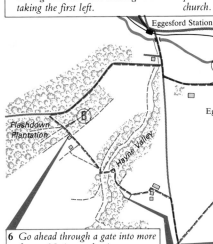

Eggesford Station   A377

(A) Church

P

Eggesford Barton

Flashdown Plantation

(B)

Hayne Valley

Lyland Wood

River Taw

6 *Go ahead through a gate into more forest. Notice a clearing on your right and turn right down it to see a plaque on your right. Retrace your steps back to the main forest track. Turn right to resume your former direction to join a road. Turn right down this road to a junction where you turn left to return to Eggesford station, or right and then left to return to your car.*

5 *Reach a fork at the edge of a forest and bear left down into the trees. The path soon swings right then bears left. Ignore the path ahead at the bend. Cross a bridge over a stream. Go ahead up a path, cross a forest track and go up into the trees for 20 yards (18 m). Fork*

right as directed by waymark arrows. After 20 more yards (18 m), fork left, as waymarked. Go uphill to a gate and ahead along an old green lane. Continue along a roughly metalled track and pass a barn on your left.

A All Saints church, Eggesford, is surrounded by wonderful views. The lack of habitations nearby means that the church is now redundant and maintained by a trust. It has a 14th-century tower and a magnificent memorial, commissioned in 1650 by Lord Chichester, to his two wives.

B This plaque commemorates the 50th anniversary of the first tree planting by the Forestry Commission in 1919.

Walk 27
TIVERTON
5.5 miles (8.9 km) Moderate

Tiverton was made prosperous in the 16th century by the wool and lace trades, and many fine old buildings have survived since then. The Grand Western Canal, which joins the river Exe here, is now a linear country park, and makes an attractive towing path walk along a wildlife corridor.

A Half-way down Gold Street, on your right, notice the Greenway Almshouses. John and Joan Greenway had these built in 1529 in order that five old men could live here and pray for the souls of their benefactors.

B The Clock Tower on your left, just after the bridge across the River Lowman, was a gift from Thomas Ford, a native of the town. He also erected the statue of King Edward VII, on your right.

C A wealthy Tudor wool merchant, Peter Blundell, founded a famous school here. Old Blundell's, the free grammar school which was completed in 1604, is now in the care of the National Trust (but you can only view the exterior from the gateway). The modern school is on the edge of the town in more spacious grounds. R D Blackmore was educated at Old Blundell's and set the opening scene of his novel *Lorna Doone* in its forecourt.

D The Grand Western Canal was an ambitious project to link the Bristol and English Channels. It was intended to run from Topsham, south of Exeter, to Taunton, to link with other navigable waterways to Bristol. The canal from Lowdwells to Tiverton was one of three projected branches of which only this one was built. Work started here, in 1810, on the summit level and where there was already a thriving local limestone trade. The 11 mile (17.7 km) canal between Tiverton and Lowdwells opened in 1814 and was chiefly used to carry limestone from the quarries at its eastern end. The main canal from Taunton to Lowdwells was not completed until 1838. With the coming of the railways the link to Topsham was abandoned, and the unprofitable Lowdwells to Taunton section was closed in 1869. The Grand Western had been reduced to a modest canal east of Tiverton. Limestone continued to be carried along it until 1924, despite the canal being owned (and poorly maintained) since 1864 by the Great Western Railway. Devon County Council finally took over the canal in 1971 and turned it into a country park. Restoration was made easier by the lack of locks, this section being on one level. Tiverton Basin was the canal's western terminus.

Notice the remains of limekilns near the tearooms in the thatched Lime Kiln Cottage at the car park. Alternative layers of limestone and coal were burnt in a brick-lined bowl, under which was a grate. The burnt lime was used in large quantities to fertilise the soil.

E Tidcombe Hall, now a Marie Curie Home, was once Tidcombe Rectory. It was built on the graveyard of a chapel.

F Unlike the canal, the railway is abandoned.

G Tiverton Museum is well worth a visit. It is open Feb - Christmas Eve Mon - Sat 10.30am - 4.30pm. Admission charge.

H Another wealthy wool merchant, George Slee, provided for these almshouses, which were built in 1613 for six poor and aged widows or maidens.

I Robert Chilcot, the nephew of Peter Blundell, built this elementary school in 1611.

J St. Peter's church includes a chapel built by John Greenway. Its outside wall is decorated with the armed merchant ships which carried Tiverton's wool abroad in the 16th century.

K Tiverton Castle dates from 1106. It is open Easter - Sep Sun - Thurs 2.30 - 5.30pm. Admission charge.

L The old Town Leat (water supply).

M The Corn Market, rebuilt in 1732.

Over

0   1 mile

0   1 km

1 *Start from the Tourist Information Centre in the car park and bus station (buses from all parts) at the end of Phoenix Lane, in Tiverton, a north Devon town situated where the A373 and A396 cross.*
Go up Phoenix Lane and turn right along Fore Street. Ignore the left fork into Bampton Street and continue along Gold Street. Cross the Lowman Bridge, marked by a clock tower, and bear right. Pass three roads on your left to reach the Grand Western Canal Country Park on your left.

6 *Continue past the church to the castle. Return to the church and turn left along Newport Street. You will continue by way of the market on your right, but first notice the old town leat in Castle Street on your left. Go left from the market to Bampton Street and turn right back to Fore Street. Return down Phoenix Lane on your left.*

2 *Turn left towards the car park, and take a path on your right to reach the canal basin. Turn left to follow the towpath with the canal on your right. Pass under a footbridge before reaching Tidcombe Bridge. Go under this road bridge to an exit on your left, turn left up the road and cross the bridge. Continue past Tidcombe Hall on your left and go left at a T junction, up Newte's Hill. Pass a lane on your left and go uphill for 0.5 mile (0.8 km).*

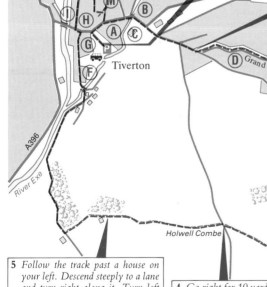

5 *Follow the track past a house on your left. Descend steeply to a lane and turn right along it. Turn left across a bridge over the River Lowman. Go along St. Andrew Street to Fore Street and go left, then right, up St. Peter Street to the parish church.*

4 *Go right for 10 yards (9 m). Then go left, across the road, over a stile beside a gate. Go down to cross another stile beside a gate and maintain your direction to join a track.*

3 *Turn right along a private road (but public path) to Gogwell. Reach a junction and go right along a hedged track to reach a road.*

This is a walk to what is considered by many to be one of the holiest spots in the West Country. The modern market town of Crediton, birthplace of St. Boniface, a great Christian saint, is a friendly place easily reached by public transport or by car. The country paths are all close by.

5 Fork right down to a road junction at Landscore School. Ignore Greenway on your right, go ahead to Threshers Road and turn left for 10 yards (9 m). Then take a passage on your right to see the ancient chapel of St. Lawrence.

Return to the road and go left to reach St. Lawrence's Green. Continue along the High Street, then Union Road, to reach a bus stop, near the war memorial, on your left.

6 Walk down the steps behind the war memorial. Go left to the statue of St. Boniface and notice the holy well on your right. Retrace your steps to Union Road and go left to the church and Libbets Well. Continue up East Street, fork right up Charlotte Street, then bear right down Exeter Road. Fork right along Four Mills Lane and go left to return to the station.

Crediton

1 Start from Crediton station on British Rail's line between Exeter and Barnstaple. Crediton is situated at the junction of the A377 and A3072. Those arriving by car or bus can start the walk near point **6**.
Go left to the level crossing, turn left to cross the railway carefully and walk away from Crediton, soon passing Brooklyn House on your left.

4 Continue over a stile and along a narrow path. Cross an estate road and pass a school on your left. Take the signposted path ahead.

3 Fork right and follow the track as it bends left past Lower Park. Bear right at a track junction and follow the track round on your right. Turn left when you reach a path junction and walk with a playground on your left. Go ahead over a stile and continue with a hedge on your right.

2 Turn right up a signposted track. Ignore a signposted path on your left when the track bears right. Go ahead carefully across the railway again and then go left.

A The chapel of St. Lawrence was built around 1200. It housed an anchorite (a hermit), suffered conversion into cottages and later fell into disrepair before the Drake family restored it.

B St. Lawrence Green was the heart of the old west town. Notice the stone socket in its centre, which is the base of the old town cross. This originally stood further up the High Street, at its junction with St. Saviour's Way, at the edge of the market. The annual fair used to be held here, with bull-baiting among the activities.

C The statue of St. Boniface was unveiled by Princess Margaret in 1960 and overlooks the holy well named after the saint.

D Crediton's parish church is an impressive building. A Saxon monastery stood here from 739, then a cathedral was built in 933, dedicated to St. Mary. The see was to stay here until 1050, when Bishop Leofric removed it to Exeter. The present church dates from the 12th century, and is called The Holy Cross. St. Boniface, who introduced Christianity to Germany, was born nearby in 680.

E Libbets Well, another holy well.

BERE ALSTON

2.5 miles (4 km) Moderate

0 ———————————————— 1 mile
0 ———————————————— 1 km

The Tamar is a winding, entrancing river when glimpsed through the attractive broadleaved trees on this walk. You are in Devon, but Cornwall is just across the river, which forms the county boundary here. The natural scenery is a superb setting for an impressive work of man – the railway viaduct. This area once used to be a hive of industry, with silver and lead mines, but now the paths are peaceful.

6 *Descend to join a lower path coming from the left. Shortly after it, on your left, are the remains of an old mine. Emerge from the trees by crossing a stile ahead.*

5 *Return into the woodland and go right, uphill. Ignore a fork going downhill on your left but bear left near the top, away from a gateway. Pass a farm above you on the right.*

4 *Bear left to walk with the River Tamar on your right. Pass cottages on your left and follow the path into woodland. Walk high above the river, then bend left with the path, take the stepping-stones across a stream and go ahead along the higher path overlooking the river. Take the lower path on your right when you reach a fork in the woods. Emerge to a magnificent view of the railway viaduct ahead.*

River Tamar

Tuckermarsh Quay

Buttspill

Station

To Bere Alston

3 *Turn sharply left and follow this track downhill for 200 yards (180 m). Pass a house on your right and reach a gateway. Go left, as waymarked, into the woods. Cross a stream and follow it down, on your right, towards the River Tamar. Ignore a path on your right as you approach the bottom of the stream's valley.*

7 *Veer slightly left uphill, as waymarked. Reach the top of the field and cross a stile to the left of a gate. Go right to follow a lane past cottages on your left. Go under the railway bridge and turn left back to the station.*

1 *Start from Bere Alston station, on British Rail's Tamar Valley Line between Plymouth and Gunnislake. Cars can be parked in the car park here. Bere Alston is signposted along minor roads to the west of Yelverton, which is on the A386 about 6 miles (9.7 km) north of Plymouth.*
Go right from the station towards the access road. Turn sharply left

2 *Continue under the old railway bridge. Ahead of you can be seen the chimney of Gawton Mine, while the view to your left is across the Tamar Valley. Go ahead along this track for 250 yards (230 m) to a junction.*

along the bridleway which runs beside the car park. Pass bungalows on your right and ignore a footpath on your left opposite the last bungalow.

A Bere Alston used to be a railway junction. The now dismantled line going east from it was the old London and South Western Railway main line, which used to speed the fruits and flowers that were grown in this valley to London's markets. Cherries, apples, pears, strawberries, plums and daffodils were all carried via Tavistock and Exeter.

B This viaduct carries the Tamar Valley Line across the river south of Calstock. It was completed in 1908 and you can still enjoy a train ride over it. Because of a problem in finding a solid foundation for one of the river piers, it took three and a half years to build. Its 11,000 blocks were made on site on the Devon side. It has a height of 117 feet (35.7 m).

C Silver came from this old mine.

Walk 30

CASTLE DROGO

6 miles (9.7 km) Moderate

A woodland path beside the River Teign, signposted as the Fisherman's Path, is contrasted by a higher route overlooking this magnificent gorge and signposted as the Hunter's Path. This is a dramatic walk full of vitality, from the sparkling waters to the scenic viewpoints. At the back of all this is a modern castle to add a sense of romance.

7 Turn left up a path signposted to Drewsteignton. Cross a stile beside a gate and walk beside a fence on your left. Go ahead over another stile and with the fence still on your left. Veer right as you approach the next field corner and cross a stile beside a gate to enter a forest. Descend through the trees to join your outward path. Go ahead back to Drewsteignton, turning right when you reach the road.

6 Retrace your steps from the castle down to the Hunter's Path. Go left along this to resume your former direction and enjoy the view across the gorge on your right. Ignore a second signposted path up to the castle on your left.

1 Start from the square in the village of Drewsteignton. This is about 16 miles (26 km) west of Exeter, signposted on a minor road to the south of the A30. Cars can be parked in the square, where the 359 bus from Exeter stops.
With the church away to your left, go ahead downhill, past the bus shelter and right towards Castle Drogo. Just after the village ends, take a path on your left signposted to Fingle Bridge.

2 Turn left at the edge of a forest, along a path signposted to Fingle Bridge. After 250 yards (225 m), fork left with the signposted path. Continue along this path to reach a road. Go right to follow this road to Fingle Bridge.

Drewsteignton

Church

Rectory Wood

Castle Drogo

Drewston Wood

Prestonbury Common

Piddledown Common

Prestonbury Castle

Whiddon Wood

River Teign

Coombe

5 Turn sharply right to go through a gate and follow the signposted Hunter's Path. Bend left with this path to continue with a fine view across the gorge on your right. Go ahead to where a signposted path on your left leads uphill to the access lane to Castle Drogo, which is on your left.

4 When you reach a metal footbridge across the river, turn right away from it. Follow the signposted Hunter's Path uphill to a rough lane. Bear right along this.

3 Don't cross the bridge. Turn right along the signposted Fisherman's Path. Follow this attractive path through woodland and beside the River Teign on your left for about 1.5 miles (2.4 km).

Over

48

A Drewsteignton has cottages with cob (a composition of clay, rubble and straw) walls under thatched roofs with brick and stone chimney stacks. These, like the church, date from the 15th century. The population peaked at 1267 in the 1830s, when there was a working lime quarry. The village is now a Conservation Area.

B Fingle Bridge dates from about 1600, when it was needed to help packhorses across the River Teign. This river rises in northern Dartmoor and is renowned for its brown trout. Look out for dippers, birds which walk under the surface of the water to catch small crustaceans.

C This path is part of the Two Moors Way, a long distance path from Ivybridge in South Devon to the North Devon coast at Lynmouth. It is 102 miles (164 km) long and crosses both Dartmoor and Exmoor.

D Castle Drogo was the last castle to be built in Britain. Standing at over 900 feet (270 m) above sea level, its granite walls are one of the most remarkable works of Sir Edwin Lutyens. Construction took nearly 20 years, from 1911 to 1930. During this time its architect was also supervising the building of the new government centre in New Delhi in India. Sir Edwin Lutyens was engaged for this castle by Julius Drewe, the founder of the Home and Colonial Stores. He wanted to own a medieval castle which offered the comforts of a modern family home. His search for his family roots led to Drewsteignton, which was named after the local lord of the manor, Drogo or Dru, a Norman. The castle provided an ancestral home. There is a mixture of styles, from Roman to Norman to Tudor. The furniture inside is an even more exotic hotchpotch, with Spanish, French, English and Norwegian. Now in the care of the National Trust, tickets for admission to the grounds, gardens and castle can be obtained at the shop in the car park. It is open Apr - Oct 11am - 6pm (closed Fri). Admission charge.

Castle Drogo

Walk 31

EXETER

4.5 miles (7.2 km) Easy

Exeter is the quintessential English cathedral city. The Romans called it *Isca Dumnoniorum* – the river town of the Dumnonii. It is a joy to walk around, and this circuitous route takes you along those narrow passages that belong to a world far away from cars. It was the River Exe that made the city great, and attractive riverside paths are followed towards the south of the city, where a canal allows ships easy access from the sea, although it is now little used.

A Notice the old city wall. This was built by the Romans in AD200, and there have been many repairs and alterations since then. The five city gates had all been demolished by 1900, to allow for road widening.

B Look for the entrance to the underground passages next to Boots. These brought water into the heart of the city during the 14th century. Open Tues - Sat 10am - 5pm. Admission charge.

C Exeter Castle was built in 1068, and its inner bailey now contains the Assize Courts of 1774. The castle is not open to the public. Do visit the nearby Rougemont House Museum, however, with its costume displays in an elegant Georgian house. Open Mon - Sat 10am - 5.30pm. Admission charge, *but free on Fri.*

D The Royal Albert Memorial Museum is known as a Victorian treasure house. Open Tues - Sat 10am - 5.30pm. Free.

E The Higher Market was designed by Charles Fowler, who also designed London's Covent Garden Market. It is now a pedestrian shopping precinct surrounding the ancient St. Pancras church.

F Look for the Ship Inn in Martin's Lane, to your right. This was said to be Sir Francis Drake's favourite inn.

G A plaque marks the site of the old South Gate where King Henry VI entered the city in 1452. It was demolished in 1819 after being used for centuries as a prison.

H Exeter was a thriving centre of the wool trade in Tudor times, using a port on the River Exe. The river was made unnavigable, however, when the Countess of Devon, Lady Isabel, built a weir 3 miles (4.8 km) south of the city. After 300 years of dispute, the city won the right to remove it, but the river had by this time silted up. The solution was for a canal to be cut by John Trew in the 1560s.

I The old canal basin is now home to the Exeter Maritime Museum. Opened in 1969, this displays boats from all over the world. Children love to clamber over the Danish steam tug, *St. Canute* from which you can look down on *Bertha*, the oldest working steam craft in the world. The great engineer, Isambard Kingdom Brunel, designed and built her in 1844. Open daily (except Christmas & Boxing Days) 10am - 5pm (6pm Jul - Aug). Admission charge.

J Quay House Interpretation Centre has static and audio-visual displays showing the history of this port. Open daily (except Christmas & Boxing Days) 10am - 5pm. Free.

K You cross a small bridge over the Higher Leat. This was one of the leats (artificial water channels) built to drain the marshes during the Middle Ages. Woollen cloth used to be fulled and dyed in this area, prior to export. The nearby Custom House dates from 1685 and is still guarded by 17th-century cannon.

L This landscaped area contains the ruin of St. Edmund's church and the magnificent bridge that was erected around 1200. It has 17 arches and is nearly 600 feet (180 m) long.

M The Tudor merchant's house was moved to the bottom of West Street on rollers in 1961.

N The chief glory of Exeter is the view of the 14th-century West Front of the cathedral. It is dedicated to St. Peter and its towers date from 1110. An abbey stood on this site from 670 and the Saxon Bishop Leofric transferred his see (area of jurisdiction) from Crediton to here in 1050.

Over

3 Reach Queen Street near Central Station (on your right) and go left. Walk to the neo-Classical façade of the Higher Market and turn right into it. Go left at St. Pancras Church, to walk along Waterbeer Street, then left along the extremely narrow Parliament Street back to the High Street.

2 Go left along the High Street and turn right up Castle Street. Enter Rougemont Gardens on your left. Walk with the castle wall on your right and go ahead through a small gateway in the adjoining city wall to enter Northernhay Gardens. Go left, downhill, through the gardens.

1 Start from the Tourist Information Centre in Exeter. This is opposite the bus station in Paris Street. There are several car parks nearby, and this route passes within yards of British Rail's Exeter Central Station at point **3**.
Go left and turn into Southernhay East on your left. When this bends left, go right and follow the signposted direction of the underground passages. Pass a remnant of the city wall on your left. Go ahead to the High Street.

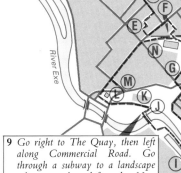

4 Go left along the High Street and turn right under an archway (St. Stephen's Bow). Turn right along Catherine Street to Cathedral Close and go left, passing the cathedral on your right, to almost reach Southernhay. Just before this road, turn right down steps signposted as a public footpath.

9 Go right to The Quay, then left along Commercial Road. Go through a subway to a landscape where you bear left under New Bridge Street, then up it and into West Street on your right. Retrace your steps to New Bridge Street, go right into Fore Street to reach the old carfax. Veer right across South Street and enter Cathedral Close. Pass the cathedral on your right, and continue to Southernhay. Turn left along it, then bear right at the end to retrace your steps to the Tourist Information Centre.

5 Follow the footpath beside the city wall, on your right, to South Street. Cross this, go left across Western Way and bear left to Holloway Street. Turn right between blocks of flats, pass the Salvation Army Temple and turn left along Colleton Crescent. Go right down Colleton Hill to The Quay.

8 Go ahead past playing fields on your left. Ignore a bridge on your right and continue to Gabriel's Wharf. Join the canal towpath which comes from your left. Go left over a bridge and turn right immediately to walk with the river on your right past the Maritime Museum on your left. Turn right across a suspension footbridge.

7 Cross the footbridge and ignore a signposted stile beside a gate on your left. Veer left across a rugby field to a cycle bridge. Cross this to take the Exe Cycle Route, going to the right on the other side of the river. Ignore a track on your left to Salmonpool Bridge over the canal.

6 Go left to walk with the River Exe on your right. Pass the Port Royal pub on your left. Go ahead along the narrow riverside path and across a footbridge passing a weir on your right. Continue along an enclosed path which veers away from the river. Ignore a path to a footbridge on your right. The enclosed path returns to the riverside, then veers away again to cross Solmonpool Lane at its corner with Old Abbey Court. Pass the polytechnic on your left and bear right down to a footbridge.

HALDON FOREST

0 ————————————————— 1 mile

0 ————————————————— 1 km

2 miles (3.2 km) Moderate

In this conifer forest, electricity power lines have provided a corridor where tall trees cannot be planted. The Forestry Commiss-ion has established a wildlife artery under the pylons and created a green waymarked Butterfly Walk, where at least 34 butterfly species have been recorded. Part of this walk follows this route. There is also much birdlife, and many wild flowers in summer.

4 Go right, as waymarked in green, at a fork. Emerge on a track just before power lines. Go left to a broader track and turn right, as waymarked in green, to pass under the power lines. Pass a coppice on your right. Turn left, as waymarked in green, onto a narrow path into the Butterfly Walk. Go downhill close to the power lines on your left. Cross a track and pass meadows on your left.

3 Bear left at a fork, where the red waymarked route joins yours. Leave the red route by turning left at a track junction marked by a green waymark post. Minor diversions may be necessary around trees that have been blown across this track. Look for a green waymark post on your left and turn left along a narrow path into the forest.

1 Start from the Information Board at the back of the car park in Haldon Forest. This is about 6 miles (9.7 km) south-west of Exeter on the A38. It can be reached by turning left just before the racecourse to go to the right under the A38, then following a lane into a forest. Ignore a turning on your left, bear left at a fork, pass the access to the Forestry Commission office on your left, then turn left along the access drive to the visitors' car park. If you rely on public transport, the nearest bus stop is at the racecourse (X39 Exeter to Plymouth bus). This is 1.5 miles (2.4 km) from the start of the walk.

With your back to the car park, take the green and blue waymarked path downhill into the forest for 20 yards (18 m), then turn right as waymarked. Veer left downhill along a narrow path.

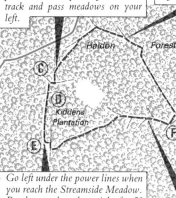

Haldon Forest

Kiddens Plantation

To the A38

5 Go left under the power lines when you reach the Streamside Meadow. Reach a track and go right for 50 yards (45 m), then turn sharply left uphill along a green-waymarked track, which may also require minor diversions around fallen trees. Rejoin the blue walk and take a narrow path to reach a broad track.

6 Go left, uphill. Ignore a converging track on your left, reach a track junction and veer left up a narrow woodland path, signposted 'return route to car park'. Pass Sitka Spruce on your left. Continue ahead to the Douglas Fir and retrace your steps past the Japanese Larch and the seat, to return to the car park.

2 Cross a track to take the waymarked path ahead. Pass toilets on your right and reach a hexagonal covered seat. Turn right as waymarked and go past Japanese Larch and Douglas Fir trees. Fork right along the green waymarked path (the blue goes ahead). This narrow path reaches a track. Go right along it and immediately fork left along a broad, firm track. Cross a brook at a right-hand bend.

A These are Japanese Larch, introduced to Britain in 1861.

B These are Douglas Fir, Britain's tallest tree, sometimes reaching 180 feet (55 m).

C This willow and birch coppice supports insects for birds to eat.

D These meadows are full of wild flowers which support butterflies.

E Streamside meadow is full of species typical of wetland soils.

F Sitka Spruce is a native of West and North America.

SIDMOUTH

0 ———————————————— 1 mile

0 ———————————————— 1 km

4 miles (6.4 km) Strenuous

The red sandstone cliffs make this a strenuous but picturesque walk. The South Devon Coast Path is well maintained, however, with plenty of steps to make short work of the climbs. You soon turn inland for gentler paths which bring you back to the coast facing towards Sidmouth, giving stunning views which may go unnoticed on the outward journey. Binoculars are useful on this walk, if you have a pair.

> **1** *Start from the bus stop (nos 52, 52A & X57 from Exeter) at The Triangle, Sidmouth. Motorists will find this seaside resort just south of the A3052 at its junction with the A375, about 10 miles (16 km) east of Exeter. There is car parking at the eastern end of the seafront, which is on the route, between points **1** and **2**.*
> *Go left towards the church of St. Giles and St. Nicholas. Turn right along Church Street. Bear right at The Market to reach the seafront. Turn left to walk with the sea on your right. The sea wall ends at an inlet. Go ahead over a footbridge and climb the steps up the cliff, to take the clifftop path past the gardens of houses on your left.*

> **5** *Reach a signpost in the corner of the field. Ignore a kissing-gate ahead and turn right over a footbridge. Veer left inland, away from the Coast Path. Go through a gate in the hedge across a corner of a field and maintain this direction to the right hand of two gates in the top corner of the next field. Go ahead to reach a waymark post. Turn left along a grassy track which becomes an access lane after Coombe Wood Farm. Ignore a signposted kissing-gate on your left. Go ahead 50 yards (45 m) and turn sharply left along the signposted path to Sidmouth.*

> **6** *Ignore a signposted path into the woods on your right. Go ahead into South Combe Farm and bear right. Go through a gate and veer right uphill to the Coast Path. Walk with the sea now on your left back to Sidmouth.*

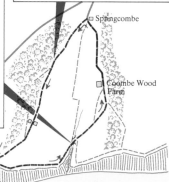

> **2** *Enter National Trust land on Salcombe Hill, where there is a hedge forming a windbreak on your right. Go inland as waymarked uphill through a copse. Reach a seat at a viewpoint over Sidmouth.*

> **3** *Fork right (but not sharp right) along the Coast Path, as signposted to Salcombe Mouth. In 50 yards (45 m) reach another signpost. Go ahead through a small gate beside a field gate, to the left of which is a toposcope indicating what can be seen from here. Enter South Combe Farm. Follow the cliff-top path above the sea on your right.*

> **4** *Go ahead through a small gate beside a field gate. Go down the waymarked steps to continue through another small gate. Follow the clifftop path to a stile in the corner of the next field. Descend to another stile in the corner of the field below it. Go ahead over this and through a signposted kissing-gate below. Ignore steps down to the beach. Pass a kissing-gate on your right and walk with a hedge on your right towards Weston Mouth.*

A Sidmouth really belongs to the 19th century. Jane Austen came on holiday here in 1801 and lost her heart to a handsome young man. Sadly, this mysterious lover was to die within weeks, leaving Jane to concentrate on writing novels.

B The toposcope near the National Trust collecting box indicates what you can see on a clear day. Berry Head is 22 miles (35.4 km) away; the Hardy Monument in Dorset is 29 miles (46.7 km) to the east.

THE DONKEY SANCTUARY

2 miles (3.2 km) Moderate

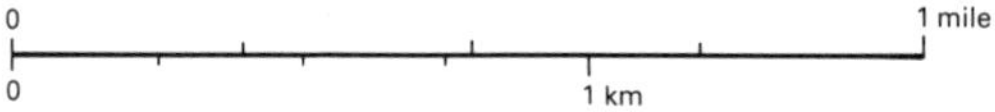

0   1 mile

0   1 km

Those who regularly walk in the country are well used to the presence of sheep and cows. This walk provides a very pleasant change – the happy sight of fields full of donkeys, rescued from toil and maltreatment and now enjoying the company of their own kind in a caring environment close to the sea. **Please** do not feed them!

1 *Start from the Donkey Sanctuary at Slade House Farm. This is just south of the A3052, about 2 miles (3.2 km) east of Sidmouth, on the lane to Branscombe. There is a car park here. An infrequent bus service passes by and will stop on request. This is Axe Valley's no 899 bus between Sidmouth and Lyme Regis. Tel: (029780) 338 for details.*
From the car park, notice the plan of the site at the rear exit, and then go left towards the hospital stables. Turn right when you are level with them to go through a gate, followed by a kissing-gate, and on down a fenced path.

2 *Cross a stile at the bottom of the fenced path and go ahead over a second stile. Turn right along a signposted path to Weston Mouth. The path descends gradually, with a hedge on your left and the wooden fence of the Donkey Sanctuary on your right.*

3 *Go ahead through two kissing-gates, then over a stile beside a gate to enter a field. Continue across this to a stile beside a gate.*

4 *Go ahead above the perimeter fence of the woodland on your left. This is at the foot of a long field. Reach a junction with a path ascending sharply to your right in its far corner.*

5 *Go left down a fenced path through the trees. Emerge in the corner of a field and keep descending beside a fence on your right. Continue along this track in the direction of the sea to reach a stile in the bottom left corner of this field, next to a signpost. Go ahead down to Weston Mouth through a nature reserve.*

6 *Admire the 533 feet (162 m) of Weston Cliff on your left and notice the Watch House. Retrace your steps up through the nature reserve to the stile. Go across it and bear left uphill, as signposted 'Coast Path Salcombe Mouth'. Walk beside a hedge and above the sea on your left.*

7 *Climb up to a waymarked stile and go over it into woodland. Go up a waymarked woodland path to a signpost and fork right towards Dunscombe. Take this narrow path to another signpost, then bear right along a concrete access track past caravans. Ignore a signposted path coming sharply from Weston Mouth on your right. Follow the concrete track as it bends left to a road at Dunscombe Manor. Turn right along this back to the Donkey Sanctuary on your right.*

Map labels: A3052 · To Sidmouth · Slade House Farm · Dunscombe Manor · Dunscombe Coppice · Weston Mouth

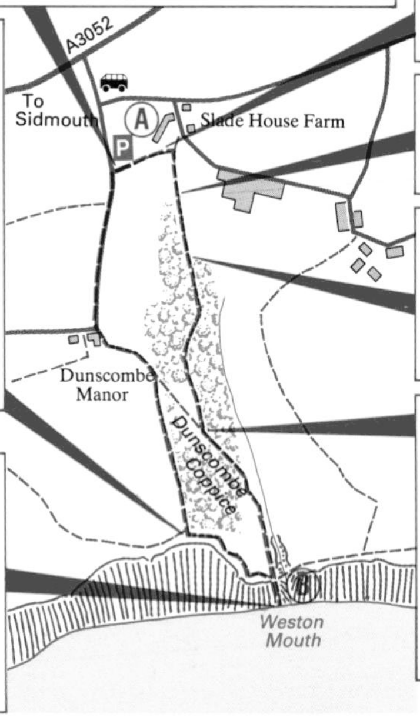

A The Donkey Sanctuary is the creation of Mrs Elizabeth Svendsen MBE and is now a registered charity. It works to rescue and care for unwanted and neglected donkeys. The Sanctuary never refuses admission to a donkey, and also maintains a team of inspectors around the country. Mrs Svendsen began her work in 1969 and moved to Slade House Farm in 1974. By 1990, over 4500 donkeys had been taken into its care. There is a Riding Centre for handicapped children. The Sanctuary is open daily all year from 9am to dusk. Free.

B Watch House at Weston Mouth is a reminder that coastguards had to be stationed here in the 18th and 19th centuries, to look out for smugglers.

BRADLEY MANOR

4 miles (6.4 km) Easy

This delightful route is well worth following at any time, with beautiful broad-leaved woodland enhancing the valley of the River Lemon. Access is easy, since the walk is on the edge of Newton Abbott, a hub of the local public transport network and a British Rail mainline station. If you wish to see inside Bradley Manor, it is open on Wednesday afternoons in summer.

4 *Continue beside the river on your left to a stile in the corner ahead. Cross it to follow a woodland path running parallel to the river on your left. Go through a gate ahead, pass a house on your right, and take a kissing-gate beside a gate to reach a road. Turn left to go over a bridge and keep left along this road, passing old lime kilns.*

3 *Go ahead along a woodland track parallel to the river on your left, then beside a channelled stream on your left. Reach a weir on your left and go ahead through a gate into a field. Walk beside the river on your left to go through a kissing-gate in the next corner. Go across a track (which leads to a ford on your left) and take a kissing-gate ahead. Pass a footbridge on your left.*

1 *Start from the car park at Baker's Park on the west side of Newton Abbot. To reach here take Wolborough Street (the A381) out of Newton Abbot in the direction of Totnes, and turn right at a telephone box down Steppes Meadow. Newton Abbot is served by trains from Exeter, Plymouth and Torquay, as well as by plenty of buses.*
From the car park, go across the bottom of the playing fields to a kissing-gate. Go through into National Trust land and bear right to cross a bridge over the River Lemon.

2 *Bear left along the access lane, ignoring a bridge and track ahead. Pass Bradley Manor on your right and continue along a rough track, with a meadow on your left. When you come to a footbridge across the river on your left, note that you will return across it. Go ahead past it for now. Continue along the track to a gate in the far corner of the meadow.*

Chercombe Bridge

River Lemon

Bradley Manor (A)

Emblett Hill

P To Newton Abbot

A381

Croft Road

East Ogwell

(B) Church

7 *Go along the signposted path through woodland, ignoring a gate into a meadow on your left. Bear left through a waymarked gate and walk with the wood on your right, then take a woodland path which climbs, forks left downhill and comes to a footbridge. Cross this and turn right to walk back to the start.*

6 *Reach the end of a row of cottages on your left, opposite Heavitree House on your right. Turn left up the lane to the church. Go over a stone stile next to a signpost and enter the churchyard. Follow the path round to the right of the church and down to a kissing-gate. Continue past tennis courts on*

your right and ahead through a kissing-gate to reach a road. Go right, past Tor Gardens on your left, then bear left up Mill Lane. Ignore a signposted path on your right. Go left with the lane downhill to a ford. Turn right just before you reach the river.

5 *Bear left towards East Ogwell when the road forks. Pass Westhill Holiday Home for Pets on your left, then turn right up Garners Close. Pass a road to West Ogwell on your right and the manor house on your left as you bend left with the road, ignoring a lane to Ipplesden on your right.*

A Bradley Manor dates from the 13th century and has some fine 17th-century panelling. Although owned by the National Trust, it is still a private house and is only open Apr - Sep Wed 2 - 5pm.

B St. Bartholomew's church, East Ogwell, also dates from the 13th century, and has a fine tower.

THE TEMPLER HERITAGE TRAIL
4.5 miles (7.2 km) Easy

This is a splendid walk, full of interest, rich in wildlife, and along well made paths. It follows the waymarked and signposted Heritage Trail, named after the first James Templer (1722-1782) who settled here after making his fortune in India. He invested in the Stover estate's right to quarry granite at Haytor. A canal and a railway were built to transport the granite, and lakes and forests were created to accompany his new house.

A Stover Country Park is now a Site of Special Scientific Interest. Bought by James Templer in 1765 as part of his estate, around 200,000 trees were planted here, including many exotic species. You will see beech, hazel, oak, sycamore and rowan, along this route, as well as squirrels, butterflies and many woodland birds.

B Stover Lake is a large ornamental lake made by diverting Ventiford Brook. It is now famous for its dragonflies and waterfowl, including tufted ducks and swans.

C This outlet channel was rebuilt in 1980.

D This is the old Moretonhampstead & South Devon Railway. Still partly open for freight, it has a long history. It opened as the Haytor Granite Tramway, horse drawn, on 16th September, 1820. Not only was it designed to carry granite from the quarries at Haytor, but it was also furnished with rails built out of granite blocks. Haytor granite was in demand for the grand buildings of the Industrial Revolution, including the British Museum, the National Gallery and London Bridge. The tramway flourished until 1858, when the quarries were closed because of competition. This tramway, and the earlier canal, were replaced in 1866 by the Moretonhampstead & South Devon Railway. Built to a broad gauge, the old granite rails were replaced with steel.

E The River Teign is noted for its herons, kingfishers and sand martins. Look out for buzzards and kestrels as well. Much of the farmland between the River Teign and the old canal is unimproved meadow. It is exceptionally rich in plant species, plus 24 species of dragonfly, badger, fox, stoat and rabbit.

F The Templer Way, which continues over the footbridge here, is about 15 miles (24 km) long. It stretches from Haytor, down the granite tramway, to the Teign Estuary at Shaldon.

G The canal was built in 1792 by James Templer junior. This was its fifth and last lock if you travelled from the Teign Estuary. Built from Haytor granite, it is 110 feet (33 m) long and was capable of accommodating two barges with a rise of 5 feet 6 inches (1.65 m). The top gate, with its balance beam and paddle gear, can still be seen. The two stone buildings on either side of the railway level crossing were part of the canal maintenance yard. James Templer junior paid for this canal to be built as a means of increasing his income from the rapidly expanding ball clay industry. This decomposed granite was formerly carried to the coast on packhorses. Until George Templer had the granite tramway built in 1820, packhorses were still used to reach the canal at Ventiford, where there was a crane to load the canal barges. It was 2 miles (3.2 km) from Ventiford to the Teign Estuary. At its peak, 10 barges each carried 25 tons of clay. These were either pulled by a man (bow-hauled) or sailed using a square rig (like Viking ships). Today, the great crested newt survives in the canal, free from commercial traffic.

H Teigngrace church was built in 1787 by James Templer's sons, James, John and George. John became the rector.

I Stover House is now a private girls' school. It was built by James Templer with granite from Haytor.

J This bridge originally crossed an ornamental pond.

Over

0   1 mile

0   1 km

3 Turn left along the signposted route of the Templer Way Heritage Trail to Ventiford. Walk beside the outlet channel on your left. Do not go ahead over a footbridge beside a cascade on your left. Turn right along a waymarked woodland path running parallel to the road on your left. Emerge through a kissing-gate to join the road at a signpost. Turn right for 20 yards (18 m), then turn left as signposted up a lane just before the Teigngrace roadsign.

2 Reach a path junction and go right along the signposted 'Templer Way Heritage Trail' towards a lake. Go across a footbridge over an inlet on your left, and walk with the lake on your right to another footbridge over an inlet. Keep to the lakeside path as it bears right to follow the northern side of the lake. Turn right to cross a footbridge over an outlet channel.

4 Cross the bridge over the railway and follow the lane to Ventiford Cottages. Turn right, as signposted, at a T junction. Follow the lane under a railway bridge to a road junction. Go left, as signposted, for 100 yards (90 m), then take the signposted path on your left to go under another railway bridge. Walk beside a stream on your left. Do not take the footbridge across it. Go ahead through a kissing-gate beside a field gate and a signpost.

5 Continue with the River Teign on your left. Bear right downstream. Ignore a footbridge on your left but go through a kissing-gate ahead and across a field.

A38

C

A

Stover
Lake

B

River Teign

D

Ventiford
Bridge

E

J

Stover School

Stover Park

I

Teigngrace

G

F

H

Stover Canal

1 Start from the Information Boards in the car park of Stover Country Park. This is about 3 miles (4.8 km) north of Newton Abbot, on your right just before reaching the A38. The nearest bus stop is served by nos 72 (Newton Abbot to Chudleigh) and 73 (Newton Abbot to Moretonhampstead). Alight at the fork in the road near Stover Bridge, where there is a bus shelter on the other side of the road. Go up the road towards the A38 for 500 yards (450 m) to reach the entrance to Stover Country Park on your right.
From the Information Boards, go left along a track signposted 'The Templer Way'.

7 Take a track on your left and follow it as it bends right to a road. Go right, as signposted, for 200 yards (180 m) then turn left along the signposted path near the 'road liable to flooding sign'. Turn right when you reach a track and follow this past the entrance to Stover School, on your left. Bear right, cross a bridge, and go ahead to rejoin your outward path at the outlet channel. Cross the footbridge to retrace your steps (with the lake now on your left) to the start.

6 Reach another footbridge. Do not cross it but bear right as signposted to a kissing-gate. Walk with the river on your left to a signpost. Turn right to reach a kissing-gate in the hedge and go ahead across the next field. Take another kissing-gate, followed by a footbridge, over a ditch. Cross the field, picking up a fence on your left after a waymark post. Follow the signposted track which bends right, then left over the Stover Canal. Continue across the railway.

Walk 37
TOTNES
4 miles (6.4 km) Easy

0   1 mile
0   1 km

Quiet paths with beautiful views over the River Dart make this a highly attractive walk. The town of Totnes is a delight in itself. The famous East Gate (also known as The Arch) was badly damaged by fire in 1990, but is being restored. You can combine this walk with a river trip or spend some time shopping. There is a costumed charity market on summer Tuesdays.

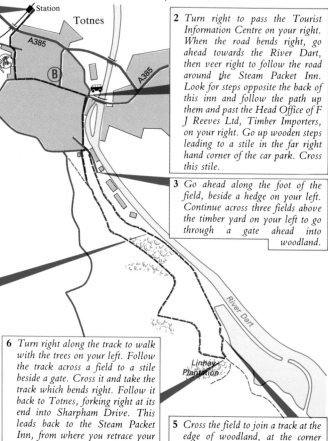

Totnes

1 *Start from the British Rail station at Totnes, which is on the main line between Plymouth and Newton Abbot. The bus station is near The Plains, at the junction of Coronation Road and Fore Street. There are several car parks close to the station. If you come by bus, join this walk at the bus stops by the Tourist Information Centre, at point **2**.*
From the railway station, go up the access road, cross the A385 and take the road ahead (Kistor Gardens, becoming Glenarm Terrace). At a junction, go ahead up a narrow path and continue to Totnes Castle, on your right. Maintain your direction along Castle Street and turn left when this joins the High Street. Pass through the East Gate and down Fore Street to The Plains.

2 *Turn right to pass the Tourist Information Centre on your right. When the road bends right, go ahead towards the River Dart, then veer right to follow the road around the Steam Packet Inn. Look for steps opposite the back of this inn and follow the path up them and past the Head Office of F J Reeves Ltd, Timber Importers, on your right. Go up wooden steps leading to a stile in the far right hand corner of the car park. Cross this stile.*

3 *Go ahead along the foot of the field, beside a hedge on your left. Continue across three fields above the timber yard on your left to go through a gate ahead into woodland.*

4 *Descend with the woodland path to the riverside. Walk with the river on your left to the end of the forest on your right, then walk up a bank to a stone stile and go ahead over it and along the foot of a field for 250 yards (230 m). Fork right, away from the river, beside a hedge on your left. Take a narrow path in the field corner ahead. Go up steps to cross a stile on your right. Continue beside a hedge on your left, over a stile and through newly-planted woodland to a gate. Go ahead through it.*

6 *Turn right along the track to walk with the trees on your left. Follow the track across a field to a stile beside a gate. Cross it and take the track which bends right. Follow it back to Totnes, forking right at its end into Sharpham Drive. This leads back to the Steam Packet Inn, from where you retrace your route to the station or bus stop.*

5 *Cross the field to join a track at the edge of woodland, at the corner where it overlooks the River Dart.*

A Totnes Castle was built in the 13th and 14th centuries with a stone keep and curtain wall. The keep stands on an 11th-century Norman mound. Now in the care of English Heritage, it is open Easter - Sep daily 10am - 6pm, Oct - Thur before Easter Tues - Sun 10am - 4 pm. Admission charge.

B When in Fore Street, look for the Brutus Stone, on your left. This is opposite Atherton Lane, a row of old cottages famous for their floral displays.

ELBERRY COVE

4.5 miles (7.2 km) Moderate

Elberry Cove and Broadsands have both played an important role in recent history. In early 1944 these beaches, fields and low cliffs where inundated with thousands of men. Not holiday-makers, but young American GIs in training. Amidst great secrecy they suddenly left, to go to the beaches of Normandy for the D-Day landings on June 6th.

> **2** *Turn right to go down a signposted path that leads to a lower road. Turn right under a railway viaduct. Continue to Broad Sands Beach, where there is a car park.*

> **3** *Take the clifftop path on your right and walk with the sea on your left. Go down steps to Elberry Cove and climb up a woodland path. Reach a junction and turn left. Continue through a waymarked gap in a wall.*

> **4** *Walk above the sea and trees on your left, and beside a hedge on your right. Emerge above Churston Cove with the breakwater of Brixham harbour visible beyond it. Reach a Recreation Path sign, and ignore an inland woodland path on your right. Go ahead along the Coast Path.*

> **5** *Reach a red arrowed signpost. Turn left to another beside a kissing-gate. Turn right, as waymarked, up a woodland path. Veer right across an open field.*

> **1** *Start from Churston station on the Torbay and Dartmouth Railway, which is joined from British Rail's station at Paignton. The 118 bus between Paignton and Brixham stops on the north side of Churston station bridge. There is a car park at point 3, Broad Sands Beach. This is 2 miles (3.2 km) south of Paignton, signposted off the A379, and motorists should join the walk here.*

From the station, go up the access road to pass The Weary Ploughman pub on your right. Cross the A3022 and go ahead along Bridge Road. Pass Fairway Close on your left. Cross a bridge over the old railway. Go left at a T junction to pass a golf course on your right and cross a bridge over the steam railway. Walk on the grass parallel to the road and pass Brakeridge Close, then Warborough Road on your left.

> **6** *Go ahead over a stone stile beside a gate and a signpost. Follow the track, ignoring a stile in the wall on your right. Reach a road, turn right and bear right at a fork. Pass a church on your left. At the next corner, where the waymark points ahead, turn left along Green Lane. Reach a road junction and turn right to walk parallel to the dismantled railway on your left back to Bridge Road, where you turn left to retrace your steps to the start.*

A The halcyon days of the Great Western Railway are evoked by the chocolate and cream carriages of the Torbay & Dartmouth Railway. The private steam trains took over when British Rail withdrew its services in 1972.

B Churston Cove was used by William of Orange to land his artillery and men on 5th November, 1688, when he came to claim the throne.

C The shaft of the old village cross is outside St. Mary's church.

BRIXHAM

4 miles (6.4 km) Easy

This walk starts from one of the most historic spots in England, where King William, Prince of Orange, made his peaceful landing to launch the Glorious Revolution in 1688. You then leave the authentic atmosphere of the old fishing harbour for the fresh breezes of Berry Head, where kittiwakes, fulmars and gulls fly around the cliffs and pink sea thrift and white rock rose may be seen in the spring. Come in the autumn to see lilac sea lavender and yellow rock samphire.

A The statue marks the spot where, on 5th November, 1688, William, Prince of Orange, afterwards William III, King of Great Britain and Ireland, landed and issued his famous declaration: 'The Liberties of England and the Protestant religion, I will maintain'. The small boat carrying William into the harbour became stuck in the mud and he was carried the last few yards on the back of a local fisherman called Varwell. Nearby can be seen the replica of Sir Francis Drake's ship the *Golden Hind*, which is open daily Easter – Sept 9am – 5pm (10pm Jul – Aug). Admission charge.

B Brixham Museum records the town's history of fishing and shipbuilding. Open Mon – Sat Easter – Oct 10am – 5.30pm. Admission charge.

C This Old Redoubt (for fortification) was built in 1804.

D The Visitor Centre has an exhibition about Berry Head. This is an outcrop of Devonian Limestone which ends abruptly in cliffs about 200 feet (60 m) high.

Brixham Harbour

Over

1 *Start from the statue of Prince William of Orange at the head of the inner harbour, Brixham. The Tourist Information Centre is nearby. A car park and the bus station are inland, 250 yards (230 m) up Middle Street, off the A3022. Brixham is served by bus nos 22 (from Kingswear) and 118* (*from Paignton, the nearest British Rail station*).
Face the statue and the harbour, and go right. Pass the Blue Anchor *and turn right up Fore Street. Turn left up Bolton Street and continue up Greenswood Road past the hospital on your left. Turn left up Castor Road.*

7 *Follow the road as it passes above the bay and the harbour on your right. Walk on from Berry Head Road into King Street. Notice Temperance Steps on your left at the bottom of King Street and* Ye Olde Coffin House *beside them. Go around to the right to return to the inner harbour and King William's statue.*

6 *Take the kissing-gate beside a signpost to go along a road which bends right down to Brixham. Pass Berry Head Hotel on your right.*

5 *Return from Berry Head to the signpost. Go right along the Coast Path past Hardy's Head Battery Viewpoint. After admiring the view across Torbay on your right, go down towards Brixham, where the long breakwater soon comes into view.*

4 *Go ahead over a stone stile and continue beside a wall on your right to reach a wooden stile. Cross this to enter Berry Head Country Park. Take the signposted Coast Path to Berry Head via Forts (C9). Go along the clifftops to the Old Redoubt, then bear left inland to the Visitor Centre near the car park. Follow the Coast Path towards the other fort on Berry Head. Reach a signpost and divert to Berry Head on your right.*

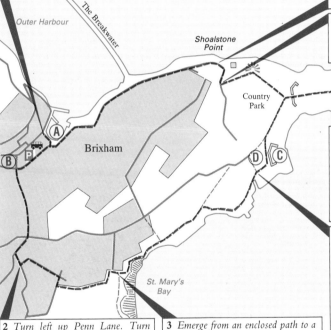

2 *Turn left up Penn Lane. Turn right when you reach Briseham Road, then take a narrow path on your left. Go over a stone stile to emerge in the corner of a field. Veer left to cross to the opposite corner and bear left, passing a holiday village on your right. Go right to follow the signposted Coast Path. Cross a stone stile and turn left along the signposted path C9 to Berry Head.*

3 *Emerge from an enclosed path to a view of Durl Head across St. Mary's Bay. Go left, walking with the sea on your right, along the clifftop path. Continue through a kissing-gate along path C9, above blackberry bushes on your right. Go ahead over a stile along the clifftop path as it passes above a cave and Durl Head. Continue to overlook two rocks out to sea, Mew Stone and Cod Rock.*

BOLT HEAD

4 miles (6.4 km) Moderate

Spectacular cliffs make this an exceptionally beautiful section of the South Devon coast. It is in the ownership of the National Trust, who have created a maze of paths.

Salcombe is the southernmost town in Devon, and exotic plants thrive here, as can be seen in Overbecks Garden. The native

wildlife is rich too, with oak and sycamore woodland, kittiwakes, sandwich terns, kestrels and a host of butterflies.

7 Go ahead along this National Trust path beside a fence on your right. Cross a stile in the field corner ahead and turn left to cross another stile and walk with a fence on your left towards South Sands. In the next corner, cross a stile on your right to follow the path down to Overbecks. Continue over another stile, ignore a path on your right to Sharp Tor and descend to the car park on your left.

6 Go left along a lane for 250 yards (230 m), then turn right along the signposted track towards East Soar Farm. Reach a stile and a signpost pointing to Salcombe Youth Hostel on your left. Turn left over it and cross a field to a stile ahead.

5 Turn right through the small gate along the signposted path to Higher Soar. Walk with a wall on your left to Middle Soar, a farmhouse, and continue along a grassy track to go through a gate in the far corner of a long field.

4 Continue through a kissing-gate, and, with the sea on your left, cross a stile beside a gate. Veer right away from the clifftops to walk with a wall on your right. Reach a signpost beside gates on your right.

1 Take the minor coast road from Salcombe harbour past South Sands for about 2 miles (3.2 km) to Overbecks Museum and Garden, a National Trust property. You may park here for a small fee.

3 Pass Bolt Head on your left, continue along the Coast Path and ignore a path back to South Sands on your right. Bear left, as waymarked, to walk parallel to a wall on your right.

From the car park, walk back down the access road to a signpost, where you turn sharply right along the Coast Path towards Bolt Head via Starehole Bay. Notice the strangely shaped rocks above you.

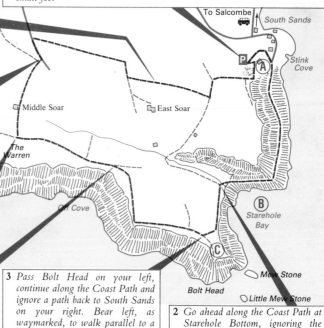

2 Go ahead along the Coast Path at Starehole Bottom, ignoring the path inland to East Soar.

A Overbecks Museum has a 'secret' room full of dolls and toys. The gardens in March are full of the pink flowers of magnolias. Museum open Apr - Oct 11am - 5pm (closed Fri). Garden open daily 10am - dusk. Admission

charge to both.

B The wreck of the *Herzogen Cecilie* can be seen in Starehole Bay. It has been here since 1936.

C Divert to inspect the World

War II look-out on Bolt Head, where you will be able to enjoy spectacular views of the coast. In late summer many thousands of swallows and house martins use this area as a migration stage.